The Princeton Review

American History
Smart Junior

Exploring America's Past

BOOKS IN THE PRINCETON REVIEW SERIES

Cracking the ACT
Cracking the ACT with Sample Tests on CD-ROM
Cracking the CLEP (College-Level Examination Program)
Cracking the GED
Cracking the GMAT
Cracking the GMAT with Sample Tests on Computer Disk
Cracking the GRE
Cracking the GRE with Sample Tests on Computer Disk
Cracking the GRE Biology Subject Test
Cracking the GRE Literature in English Subject Test
Cracking the GRE Psychology Subject Test
Cracking the LSAT
Cracking the LSAT with Sample Tests on Computer Disk
Cracking the LSAT with Sample Tests on CD-ROM
Cracking the MAT (Miller Analogies Test)
Cracking the NTE with Audio CD-ROM
Cracking the SAT and PSAT
Cracking the SAT and PSAT with Sample Tests on
    Computer Disk
Cracking the SAT and PSAT with Sample Tests on CD-ROM
Cracking the SAT II: Biology Subject Test
Cracking the SAT II: Chemistry Subject Test
Cracking the SAT II: English Subject Tests
Cracking the SAT II: French Subject Test
Cracking the SAT II: History Subject Tests
Cracking the SAT II: Math Subject Tests
Cracking the SAT II: Physics Subject Test
Cracking the SAT II: Spanish Subject Test
Cracking the TOEFL with Audiocassette
Flowers & Silver MCAT
Flowers Annotated MCAT
Flowers Annotated MCATs with Sample Tests on
    Computer Disk
Flowers Annotated MCATs with Sample Tests on CD-ROM

Culturescope Grade School Edition
Culturescope High School Edition
Culturescope College Edition

LSAT/GRE Analytic Workout
SAT Math Workout
SAT Verbal Workout

All U Can Eat
Don't Be a Chump!
How to Survive Without Your Parents' Money
Speak Now!
Trashproof Resumes

Biology Smart
Grammar Smart
Math Smart
Reading Smart
Study Smart
Word Smart: Building an Educated Vocabulary
Word Smart II: How to Build a More Educated Vocabulary
Word Smart Executive
Word Smart Genius
Writing Smart

American History Smart Junior
Astronomy Smart Junior
Geography Smart Junior
Grammar Smart Junior
Math Smart Junior
Word Smart Junior
Writing Smart Junior

Business School Companion
College Companion
Law School Companion
Medical School Companion

Student Advantage Guide to College Admissions
Student Advantage Guide to the Best 310 Colleges
Student Advantage Guide to America's Top Internships
Student Advantage Guide to Business Schools
Student Advantage Guide to Law Schools
Student Advantage Guide to Medical Schools
Student Advantage Guide to Paying for College
Student Advantage Guide to Summer
Student Advantage Guide to Visiting College Campuses
Student Advantage Guide: Help Yourself
Student Advantage Guide: The Complete Book of Colleges
Student Advantage Guide: The Internship Bible
Hillel Guide to Jewish Life on Campus
International Students' Guide to the United States
The Princeton Review Guide to Your Career

Also available on cassette from Living Language
Grammar Smart
Word Smart
Word Smart II

The Princeton Review

American History
Smart Junior

Exploring America's Past

by James L. Alouf

Random House, Inc., New York 1997

Princeton Review Publishing, L.L.C.
2315 Broadway, 3rd Floor
New York, NY 10024
E-mail: web-info@review.com

ISBN 0-679-77357-6

Designed by: Illeny Maaza
Edited by: Bronwyn Collie

Manufactured in the United States of America on recycled paper.
9 8 7 6 5 4 3 2 1

Acknowledgments

I would like to acknowledge Tim Egnor, Social Studies Coodinator for Volusia Country Public Schools, Daytona Beach, Florida; Ron Hegedus, middle-school teacher in Montgomery County, Maryland, and Debbie Powell and Dick Needham at the University of Northern Colorado, Greeley, for sharing ideas and information. I truly appreciate your friendship.

I would also like to thank some very special people who have provided unconditional support to this endeavor. They are John D. Currier, Jr., Wm. A. Little, Bronwyn Collie, Michael Bentley, and Maurine Harrison. These friends have never stopped believing in me and I am truly grateful for their love and support. I would also like to thank Jeff Moores for drawing the illustrations, Illeny Maaza for designing the book, John Bergdahl for drawing the timelines, and John Pak and Brendan Milburn for their production work. Thank you all.

DEDICATION

This book is dedicated to the memory of my father, Fredrick K. Alouf, who loved American History. Dad would spend hour after hour with a stamp collection that he started when he was nine years old—he developed that hobby for over fifty years. He loved those stamps and the history that went with them. He was the first historian I ever knew.

This book is also dedicated to my mother, Geneva Britt Alouf, who has always loved and supported me in all my endeavors. She has always encouraged me to live up to my fullest potential as a person. Thanks, Mom, for being there when I needed you.

My parents lived through much of the American history that is in this book. They knew the joys and hardships of growing up in an America where everyone worked together just to survive. They valued education and perseverance. I will always be grateful to them for sharing their lives with me.

CONTENTS

Introduction

Welcome! Welcome to the continuing adventures of Bridget, Babette, Barnaby, and Beauregard as they explore America's past. Wait! The past is not boring! It's full of people, places, and events that are incredibly exciting! I know, you've heard that one before. Well, not this time! You've never had the opportunity to *meet* Ben Franklin or Thomas Jefferson, have you? You see, this book is not a boring textbook or a lecture. It's an adventure story where you talk with famous people, visit exciting places, and attend important events in American history. Imagine that! Better yet, there's no pressure to learn history to pass a test. The idea behind this book is to learn some history while you enjoy the adventures of the past.

Be warned, however, that you might be doing some thinking along the way. Thinking is not memorizing. Thinking in history means developing different perspectives, collecting evidence, and making decisions. When you read history, you see how other people decided to live their lives and how those lives worked out. You get to think about the decisions that they made, too. Would you have made the same choices?

So, you'll find quizzes to help you check your progress and questions that challenge you to think. There are also group activities that you'll enjoy because they give you some good suggestions for things you can *do*. You see, history is not something old and dull. History is life itself. So, enjoy the time adventures of Bridget, Babette, Barnaby, and Beauregard while you read about America's past. And maybe, just maybe, you'll find yourselves saying, "I *love* history!"

Other Stuff that's Worth Noting

You might enjoy keeping a journal to write down your thoughts and reactions to America's past. You'll find some questions that you can answer in your journal at the end of every chapter. But remember, there are lots of possible reactions, so don't look for the answers in the back of the book! You will find answers to the quizzes in the back, however, as well as a list of all of America's presidents for handy reference. There are timelines at the beginning of each chapter, too. Look for the names of famous people and events from the chapter in chronological order. You might find a few surprises! You might also like to find important people and events that aren't mentioned in the chapter, just for fun!

Now, you're ready to get started. Enjoy *American History Smart Junior!* It was written with you in mind.

Chapter 1
Curiosity Almost Kills the Cat!

I *love* history. After all, I come from a long line of well-bred aristocrats from South Carolina whose ancestry goes back to the early days of colonial independence. Why, my great, great, great, great grandfather Beaufort was actually involved in a skirmish or two during the Revolutionary War. Oh, but excuse me. I have failed to introduce myself properly. My name is Beauregard, and I am a gentleman cat whose good manners and size—over four feet tall when standing upright —are legendary. You might also take note of my elegant, glossy black fur, my immaculately groomed paws, and my incredible talent for sensing trouble in the making.

Well, I must admit, those cute young humans almost had me meeting my ancestors in the fur! It all started one beautiful spring afternoon in New York City. I was visiting a young feline friend, a remarkably beautiful red tabby named Tallulah, whom I hadn't seen in years. We were just about to partake of a little fish-head mousse when I spotted my favorite humans, Bridget, Babette, and Barnaby, crossing the street beneath Tallulah's balcony. I was so surprised to see them that I departed from my usual luncheon manners and stretched between the railings to overhear their conversation. You wouldn't believe what a mistake that turned out to be!

✎ ✎ ✎ ✎ ✎

"You Americans are incredible!" cried Babette. "I am so curious to learn more about the American crock pot. Isn't that what you call your cultural heritage?"

"You mean melting pot, not crock pot," replied Bridget, trying not to laugh. "Yep, we call it a melting pot. I'm not sure why, but I bet Barnaby knows," she challenged.

Barnaby did not appear to be listening to their conversation. He was staring at the skyscrapers, noting the velocity of the wind down the canyons of the city streets. "I'll have to develop a wind sock to measure the wind direction," he thought excitedly. Then, suddenly, he sat down and began to remove his shoes. Babette and Bridget gasped and shouted simultaneously, "No way!"

Babette looked at Barnaby as if she already smelled something foul. In fact, you could tell she was ready to assume a karate attack position. "Do you not remember, Barnaby, that your socks are lethal weapons?" she gasped. "The last time we met, your sock collection created a violent explosion!"

"That's right," Bridget choked. "Keep your shoes on and save the city from an ecological disaster!" Bridget can be a little gruff sometimes.

Suddenly, the three kids caught a glimpse of a familiar figure above their heads, an enormous black cat whose elegant demeanor left them all speechless. Could it be Beauregard? Who else could it be? They were so pleased to see him that, although he appeared to be preoccupied at the moment, they couldn't help but to create a scene on the city street.

_____

Well, I could not believe my eyes and ears. This moment must be the epitome of serendipity: My companions in adventure were right beneath my feet! Babette's black ensemble with bright red lipstick, Bridget's Yankee's baseball cap and bubble gum, and Barnaby's lab coat and wild, bushy hair were exactly as I'd remembered. I smelled it again, though. Yep, trouble.

It follows those kids like an aardvark to an anthill. Reluctantly, I excused myself from my delightful company, having decided I'd better stick the kids around for a while to see if I could prevent disaster. Too late. Bridget was talking about a balloon trip.

✎ ✎ ✎ ✎ ✎

After they had recovered from the surprise of finding themselves all together again, it seemed strange that the group would merely hang out like three ordinary people and a talking cat. As might be expected, they began to get a little fidgety.

"I'm getting bored with all of this hanging out and stuff," said Bridget. "Isn't it time for a little action? Where do you want to go to soak up a little culture, Babette?"

Babette sighed, "Ah, you Americans are so direct. There are so many places to visit, but there is one symbol that America and France have in common. It was a gift to the United States from the people of France on the centennial anniversary of American independence."

"You must mean the Statue of Liberty," Bridget quipped. "I think this calls for a reunion balloon expedition. It's been a while since I've done this balloon thing, so get ready for a ride!"

Bridget's bubble gum was working overtime. She began to blow a huge bubble that gradually lifted her off the ground. As she floated upward, Babette and Barnaby each grabbed a leg. Then, as Beauregard's paws wrapped around Barnaby's legs, the bubble balloon grew even bigger, went even higher.

They sailed past the Empire State Building, the World Trade Center, and out into New York Harbor, the city skyline flashing with all the colors of the rainbow. Babette cried, "It's Emerald City!" as images of sky, water, and sunlight were reflected in the mirrored surfaces of the cityscape. Ahead of them in the harbor stood one of America's most cherished, most beautiful monuments, the Statue of Liberty.

"She must be three hundred feet tall," Barnaby estimated as they came in to land at the base of the statue's pedestal. "Judging from her color, she must be made of copper, which oxidizes to a blue-green hue over time."

"She is certainly one of the most beautiful monuments I have ever seen," an awestruck Babette responded. "Ah, but then her origins are French, correct?"

Bridget smiled and retorted, "Look, Frenchie, don't get carried away just yet, okay? We've got tons of places to go and loads of cool things to see. We're just getting started!"

None of the kids saw Beauregard head inside the pedestal; all three were too busy staring up at the statue's torch, high above their heads.

"Where's Beauregard?" Bridget asked a while later. "I don't see him anywhere...and he always sticks pretty close by," she added nervously.

They started looking around the grounds of Liberty Island. Had he gotten lost? Not likely. Is he playing hide-and-seek? That's hard to imagine! Catnapped? Gloriosky, somebody's got Beauregard! And by now the day had flown by and the park was about to close. You never seem to have enough time when you really need it.

The last place they looked was inside the pedestal itself. Facing them as they entered was a beautiful plaque with a poem, but no one was in the mood to read it. Later, maybe, once their feline friend had been recovered.

On the far side of the room, Barnaby saw what appeared to be a barricaded staircase. There was a curtain pulled partially across the entrance, blocking the public eye from getting a clear view. His curiosity got the better of him.

"I'll bet that's where he is," he concluded. "After all, this is an island and he's got to be here somewhere."

Bridget nudged Babette sharply. "What is wrong *now*?" Babette asked. They were all feeling pretty agitated.

"Over there, in the corner, there's a guy who looks like a cross between Albert Einstein and Barnaby watching us. He looks pretty scary to me. Kind of like some mad scientist with poor hygiene. Let's get out of here before he decides he wants to experiment on us!"

It was too late. Barnaby had spotted the man and was hurrying toward him, his arms flinging about in open admiration. "Dr. Tempus Fugit, I'd recognize you anywhere! Your research in quantum mechanics and time theory has been an inspiration to me," he announced effusively.

Babette and Bridget looked at each other with astonishment.

"I guess our Einstein and Barnaby know each other," Bridget said with relief as Babette relaxed herself from combat readiness. They joined Barnaby, awaiting introduction.

Before Barnaby could speak another word, however, Dr. Tempus Fugit said, "You young people are looking for a large black cat with a moist nose and groomed paws, aren't you? Come with me!"

They all started toward the barricaded staircase in hot pursuit of Dr. Tempus. He shuffled along at an incredible rate, almost like a guy who walks around in bedroom slippers all day. Down the stairs they flew, anxious to be reunited with Beauregard who had been missing for several hours now. They ended up in a large hall lined with a bank of sophisticated computers and what appeared to be some sort of telemetry equipment. But no sign of Beauregard!

Barnaby sputtered to life. "I've never seen so much hardware in one spot. You must be working on something top secret, something really important!"

For the first time, Babette, Bridget, and Barnaby got a good look at Dr. Tempus Fugit. He had a hairdo that made him look like an aging refugee from Generation X. It wasn't spiked or mohawked or green or red. It was white, snow white, and it stuck out all over his head. He wore wire-rimmed glasses on the end of his hairy nose. His mustache was a remarkable handlebar, unruly, and as white as his hair. Could it be Jerry Garcia's older brother or Barnaby's grandfather? His lab coat was stuffed with papers covered with mathematical formulas. His eyes were a soft brown, wise, contemplative, and full of life. He seemed annoyed at the moment, which you could tell by the way his nose and ears were twitching uncontrollably.

"Your friend is quite a nuisance, I tell you," the doctor started. "He's got great spy potential. Has he done that sort of work before?"

Bridget was now beside herself with worry. "What's happened to Beauregard? Why haven't we seen him for hours?" she snapped.

The doctor simply smiled and said, "Come, be my guest. I'll give you a tour of my latest invention, *Lady Liberty.*"

The doctor's evasiveness left the trio uneasy. He led them toward a darkened corner of the great room where a projectile of some sort had been draped with a large tie-dyed drop cloth. As he approached, light bathed the area like a launch pad at Cape Canaveral. Dr. Tempus grabbed a remote and began pressing the buttons furiously.

"Can I be of assistance?" Barnaby inquired.

"Yes, er, yes you can, young man," the doctor responded. "Kindly push this button while I tug on that drop cloth. Ready? One, two, three, PUSH! The cloth cleared the top of the gantry to reveal a miniature version of the Statue of Liberty.

"Pleeeaasse explain to me why I'm standing in some lunatic's laboratory when I started out looking for Beauregard," Bridget exploded.

No sooner had those words left her mouth than the sleek, classy form of the mannerly cat appeared, complete with technician's lab coat and chef's hat.

"Why, he's been preparing dinner on board *Lady Liberty,*" Dr. Tempus replied. "He assured me that he was a gourmet cook and he *knew* you'd all be starving. So I thought, why not surprise you all?"

Babette, Bridget, and Barnaby yelled in unison, "Beauregard!" and ran to greet their friend with strokes and nuzzles.

"It's about time you got here! My dinner is nearly ruined," Beauregard responded casually.

The group moved excitedly toward the launch pad and climbed through the narrow hatchway and into the galley, ready to feast. Beauregard had thoughtfully avoided his own delicacies like mousetail stew and entrecote of rat and instead had prepared a platter of burgers, a few hot dogs, fries, and ice cream for dessert. Gourmet, indeed!

Barnaby was eating and talking at the same time. He was full of questions, mostly about *Lady Liberty*'s instrumentation and ultimate purpose. The good Dr. Tempus looked cautiously around the cabin before responding.

"The walls have ears, you know," he said secretively. "We must not be overheard. Beauregard's snooping almost cost me a major security breach. This is top secret work! Are you all trustworthy?"

"Do we look like spies?" Bridget quipped. "C'mon, Dr. Tempus, we're just three ordinary kids."

"Well," Dr. Tempus began. "My radar screens picked you up as you floated in for a landing, which didn't look too ordinary to me. Then again, I'm not really up with the way kids are getting around these days—it's taken me *years* to develop my latest invention. Naturally, I thought you might be trying to spy. After all, we are sitting in the first time machine ever invented!"

A stunned silence fell over the group. Time travel! So Dr. Tempus Fugit had discovered one of the most jealously guarded secrets in all the universe. Human beings have longed for the ability to traverse time and space. So many of the earth's great mysteries could be investigated. People could find out about the origin of the human species, how the pyramids of Egypt were built, or visit their ancestors in order to check out their own personal histories. The possibilities were endless!

"Of course, I've never really tested her out but she's ready to roll once I get a test crew brave enough to take a short trip back in time. You see, I am not prepared to live the future until I know more about the past."

Barnaby had been silent long enough. "Why?" he asked. "Why would anyone want to know what's already known when they could know the future? If I want to know about the past, I can read a history book. If I want to surmise about the future, I can read fiction. History is fact, the future is fiction, wouldn't you agree, Dr. Tempus?"

Dr. Tempus stared into empty space, collecting his thoughts. "Why do you assume that history is fact, Barnaby? In saying that history is fact, are you suggesting that history is the truth? Do facts really change?"

Babette leaned forward in her chair, anxious to participate. "If all history books were true, why would there be so many of them to read? There would be just one or two books, correct? In France, I read many books, sometimes about the same subject. We talk about how the author's point of view influences what she writes. The author's perspective does influence what she writes, correct?"

Bridget chimed in before Dr. Tempus could respond. "Yeah! What Babette is saying makes a lot of sense. American history from an African American perspective is way different from a Native American perspective."

"Sooooo many questions, so little time!" Dr. Tempus Fugit cried. "Let's take things a bit slower. It is true that there are many history books, each with a different perspective of the past. And that's not a weakness, it's a strength! Suppose I want to write a history of my family. I seek out historical records—diaries, journals, photographs, newspapers—all of which amount to records of my family's lives and how they lived them. If I selected any one of these artifacts would I do a better job of understanding my family's past or would it be better to use as many of these sources as possible?"

Bridget had been squirming. Finally, she spoke up. "This conversation is getting a little heavy, isn't it? I mean, what's your point? Sure, I'd get a much better picture of my family by using all the resources I could find. I see a different problem. What if I don't have anything to use?"

Barnaby jumped up excitedly. "Yes, that is a problem. In science, we get to repeat experiments to see if we get the same results. Historians can't do that."

Dr. Tempus smiled and said, "Well, I see the parallel in some ways because historians are always looking for the reasons why an event occurred and they eliminate the possibilities based on the evidence available to them. Still, how much evidence is enough? How do they know that their sources are reliable or accurate?"

"I'm getting a headache from this discussion," Bridget complained. "Tell us the answer and let's talk baseball before I start to nod off."

"Maybe he's suggesting that historians seek the truth but they don't always find it," Babette mused. "Since people have different perspectives about why something happened, maybe if we collected as many different points of view as possible, we'd actually know more than if we read only one point of view. We could argue both sides of an issue and see why people made the decisions they made. That makes sense to me."

"I see what you mean, Babette!" Barnaby announced, his hair suddenly expanding to new heights. "The more history I know, the better informed I am! I can see the problems people faced in the past and how they chose to solve them. I can see what worked and what didn't. I can make better decisions for myself and for my country!"

Without warning, Barnaby's hair produced a flood of tiny American flags and a small record player blaring a rendition of John Philip Sousa's famous "Washington Post March." The humans all jumped to their feet and marched dramatically around the cabin of *Lady Liberty*, flags in hand, singing along with the music.

Beauregard had curled up under the table for a short nap while all the discussion was going on. After all, he did cook dinner.

Somebody else would have to clean up! Unfortunately, he awoke somewhat suddenly in the midst of some sort of patriotic fervor, flags waving, humans marching. And someone marched right on his tail!

There was an eardrum-rupturing growl, as if Jurassic Park had suddenly come indoors. Beauregard bolted from under the table, tail in paws, and landed right on Dr. Tempus Fugit's lap. The doctor shrieked, "I knew it! He's after me and my time machine! He's a spy!"

Mayhem erupted in the main cabin of *Lady Liberty*. Dr. Tempus dashed for the exit, dumping Beauregard, overturning the table, and throwing Bridget, Barnaby, and Babette onto the floor. Without warning, the door sealed and a dim red light filled the cabin.

"Remain still and touch nothing until I return!" Dr. Tempus shrieked hysterically. "I'm going to the authorities! We'll get to the bottom of this spy business once and for all!"

"Wha—what happened?" Barnaby asked. "Where's Dr. Tempus?"

"He flew the coop and this place is giving me goosebumps," Bridget responded. "He thinks Beauregard attacked him, but I think somebody stepped on Beauregard's tail while we were partying to the music. I want to get out of here!"

Babette spoke sharply, "Do not panic. Chill out, as you say in this country. One false move and we could end up meeting Godzilla in the flesh! Barnaby, do you think you can find the light switch? I cannot see with my sunglasses on."

Barnaby struggled to his feet. He could barely see, but he had noticed all kinds of notebooks on the shelf by the control panel in the main cabin. He headed for the shelf. "I've found it...I think."

Before anyone could speak, Barnaby threw the switch. The drone of a thousand bumble bees filled the cabin. The lights flickered momentarily, then white light flooded the interior of the machine.

"That wasn't the *light* switch, that was the *launch* switch!" Babette yelled over the increasing drone of the time-warp drive. "Quick! Turn it off!"

Barnaby lunged for the switch but he was too late. He was thrown backward abruptly as *Lady Liberty*'s auto pilot took command of the ship.

"I think we're about to launch!" he yelled.

The new crew of the time machine scrambled quickly to their chairs and strapped themselves in.

Dr. Tempus Fugit heard the primordial hum of the time-warp drive as he approached his laboratory. The guards who accompanied him hurried ahead as he shuffled quickly down the stairs into the open work space where *Lady Liberty* stood. As they watched, the time ship shimmered like a desert mirage and vanished from view without a trace!

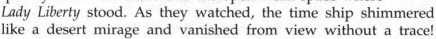

No doubt you are surprised that I have had little to say throughout the previous scenario. You realize, of course, that I told you about these young humans and trouble. I did not expect Dr.Tempus Fugit to be such a scaredy cat, if you'll excuse the expression. My reaction was purely reflex, with no intention to harm but perhaps to indicate my displeasure with his thoughtless behavior. But there are a few more details you should know.

I did sneak aboard the time machine before Dr. Tempus even knew I was around. I read everything I could get my paws on, including how to set the year of destination with a device called a tempometer, named after Dr. Tempus himself. The doctor's biggest plan, however, was to make time travel a tourist attraction! Why clone dinosaurs if you could visit them for real? Imagine the possibilities of a vacation in the past—the famous people you could meet, the major events you could attend, the places you could see! He saw one major problem: Would time travelers change the course of history as we now know it? If they changed history, would they eliminate themselves from the present? Wouldn't that be an interesting result of your summer vacation? You return to the present to find out that you never existed! Maybe you'd be a permanent resident of the Bermuda Triangle or an uninvited guest star in a horror movie. Personally, I wouldn't mind reliving a few of my own former feline flings, just to refresh my memory, of course. But, I digress.

You may not realize it, but *Lady Liberty* gave New York City quite a jolt when she shot out of the torch of the real Statue of Liberty. It felt like a space shuttle launch without the sound. Everything vibrated like a tuning fork for a few seconds, and then, silence.

✍ ACTIVITIES ✍
The Time Traveler's Guide to the Past

Try a few of the following activities with your family or friends. They will help you reflect about your reading so far. Don't be afraid to ask questions. After all, history can help us figure out the best questions to ask!

1. If you like to write or draw, keep a journal as you read this book. The journal could be a notebook, a computer file, a sketch pad, or any combination of media you prefer. Use it whenever you want to respond to a question or to ask questions of your own.

2. If you could join the "crew" of *Lady Liberty*, where would you want to go? Who would you like to meet? What events would you like to check out for yourself? Why?

3. Suppose your history class is starting the year with a debate. The teacher writes the following sentence on the board: "Those who fail to understand history are doomed to repeat it." Do you agree or disagree with this statement? What evidence can you use to support your position?

4. In your opinion, what is the difference between history and historical fiction? How can you tell the difference between the two? Can you give an example of each?

5. Do facts change? What would cause a fact to change? Do historical facts change?

1600

1607 ▶ First permanent English settlement in America

1776 ▶ Declaration of Independence written

1789 ▶ U.S. Constitution ratified

1791 ▶ Bill of Rights ratified

1803 ▶ Louisiana Purchase

1812 ▶ War of 1812

1835 ▶ Trail of Tears

1860 ▶ Lincoln becomes president

1861–1865 ▶ Civil War

1877 ▶ Reconstruction ends

1896 ▶ Henry Ford utilizes the assembly line in automobile manufacturing

1903 ▶ Wright Brothers fly at Kitty Hawk, N.C.

1914–1918 ▶ World War I

1920 ▶ Nineteenth Amendment gives women the right to vote

1923 ▶ Teapot Dome Scandal revealed; Harding dies in office and Coolidge assumes presidency

1924 ▶ Calvin Coolidge elected president

1928 ▶ Herbert Hoover elected president

1929 ▶ Stock market crash and the Great Depression begins

1932 ▶ Franklin D. Roosevelt becomes president, announcing a "New Deal" for Americans

1939 ▶ World War II begins in Europe

1941	United States enter World War II following Japanese attack on Pearl Harbor
1944	D-Day invasion of Normandy
1945	End of World War II; Atomic bombs dropped on Japan
1948	Harry Truman elected president
1950	Korean war begins
1952	Dwight Eisenhower elected president
1953	Stalin dies; Korean War ends
1954	Brown vs. Board of Education decision by Supreme Court
1963	John F. Kennedy assassinated, Lyndon B. Johnson becomes president; Civil rights march on Washington where Rev. Dr. Martin Luther King Jr. delivers "I Have A Dream" speech
1968	Rev. Dr. Martin Luther King Jr. and Robert Kennedy assassinated
1969	First Moon landing
1973	Richard Nixon resigns the presidency following the Watergate Scandal; Gerald Ford replaces him
1976	Jimmy Carter becomes president
1980	Ronald Reagan becomes president
1988	U.S. budget deficit reaches $2.3 trillion
1989	Berlin Wall torn down
1990	Saddam Hussein invades Kuwait
1992	Bill Clinton elected president

Chapter 2
The Colonists Rule!

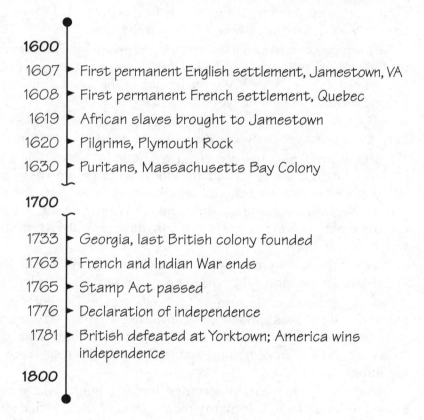

1600
1607	First permanent English settlement, Jamestown, VA
1608	First permanent French settlement, Quebec
1619	African slaves brought to Jamestown
1620	Pilgrims, Plymouth Rock
1630	Puritans, Massachusetts Bay Colony

1700
1733	Georgia, last British colony founded
1763	French and Indian War ends
1765	Stamp Act passed
1776	Declaration of independence
1781	British defeated at Yorktown; America wins independence

1800

"Where are we anyway?" Bridget grumbled as she fought to free herself from her chair. "I feel like I've watched too many episodes of *Star Trek*. That time-warp drive sure leaves you feeling pretty weird. Are you guys all right?"

Babette was still recovering from the warp-drive light show. "I believe I am fine," she answered, "but I'd like the license plate of the truck that hit me. Barnaby, can you figure out how to get us home? I wish you had thought twice before you threw that switch!"

Barnaby had struggled to his feet, his hair wilder than ever. "Incredible! We've become time travelers! We'll all be famous and make millions of dollars like Steven Spielberg or George Lucas! We're the pioneers of time travel!"

"Get a grip, Barnaby," Bridget snapped. "We won't have a future until we figure out how to get back to the present. Do we have any way of knowing where we are right now?"

"It's 'up periscope' time!" Barnaby cried excitedly. He scrambled up the ladder to the eyes of *Lady Liberty*, pressed the viewer, and looked out at the past. "Well, we're still in the United States, but I don't believe we're in New York City anymore."

Bridget was getting restless and hungry. "I'm ready for a snack and some exercise. Anyone care to join me for an outing?"

Barnaby scratched his head and a few candy bars fell out of his hair. "Before we head out the door, we'd better know more about where we've landed. Let's eat these while we look for some sort of beginner's guide to time travel. Wait! Eureka! I bet all the information we need is stored in the computer. I'm sure I can figure it out."

"Cool! I think I'll enjoy a little snack relief, then we can figure out where we are and what we're going to do next," Bridget said.

Beauregard had curled up at Bridget's feet for a short catnap; the atmosphere was amazingly calm after such a crazy journey. But suddenly, there was a loud knock at the main cabin door. Everyone bolted upright and naturally, Babette was ready for anything.

"Anybody home? Mighty strange looking home you got. I'm knocking on doors to inform my fellow citizens that Patrick Henry is delivering a speech tonight. Rumor is, he's calling for arming the Virginia militia against the British. It's a time for public discussion and debate and you may wish to participate! Hear ye! Hear ye! If they ask who sent you, tell them it was the town crier."

"Well, it strikes me that we've just received all kinds of clues as to our whereabouts, but we'd better find out who Patrick Henry is before we step out that door," said Barnaby. "What's a 'town crier' anyway?"

Bridget looked surprised for a moment, then responded. "He's like the old-time equivalent of the telephone. When there were no phones, towns had guys who roamed around ringing bells and making PSAs for a living. During colonial times, I guess they were pretty popular, especially in small towns. You don't know who Patrick Henry is?" Bridget had this look on her face that said, "You're slipping, pal."

"What are PSAs? Who is Patrick Henry?" Babette's sunglasses had slipped down to the end of her nose.

Barnaby's response was somewhat to the point. "Public service announcements, you know, as on radio and television. Patrick Henry? Well, I guess I do remember something about him. He's one of the Founding Fathers, and we have a chance to see him speak if we can just figure out how to do it!"

Barnaby scratched his head. Babette and Bridget giggled because they *knew* something would fall out. What would it be this time? Well, they couldn't eat it. It appeared to be a handbill of some sort.

"It's the colonial equivalent of a PSA! There's a date on it, too," Barnaby said excitedly. "We're in Richmond, Virginia, and it's March 23, 1775. We're over two hundred years away from home! Patrick Henry is speaking tonight at St. John's Church before the Virginia revolutionary convention. We want to be there!"

"Why? Why do we want to be there? Does this speech have some cultural significance?" Babette didn't like to feel unprepared for a big event.

"Okay, Barnaby, this is your ballpark," Bridget replied. "We know where we are and we know that we need more information. We need to get down to some serious history! We've got too many questions and too few answers!"

"I agree wholeheartedly," Barnaby said calmly. "Let's see if I can surf the computer's memory for some more background information."

Barnaby headed to the main computer console to do a search. "What descriptors should I use?" he called over his shoulder.

"How about 'American Revolution' for a start?" Bridget called back.

"Once we have a little background, we can get down to a few specifics."

"This computer has loads of information! I've asked for a summary. You'll have it in your hands in a few minutes, if I read the menu correctly," Barnaby said.

Sure enough, a couple of minutes later, the kids were reading about the American Revolution.

THE ORIGINS OF THE AMERICAN REVOLUTION 1607-1733

New England Colonies

Massachusetts (colonized by the Pilgrims and the Puritans between 1620 and 1630); Rhode Island (founded in 1636 by Roger Williams); Connecticut (founded in 1633 by Thomas Hooker); New Hampshire (founded in 1623 by John Mason).

Social Organization

Towns were founded by church groups; church leaders gave land to settlers; the town was the focal point of life in New England. Since they lived close together, New Englanders had a strong group identity. They also had a strong tradition of schooling.

Environment

Long winters, short growing season, and rocky soil. Farms tended to be small, and close to town.

Middle Atlantic Colonies

Virginia (Jamestown was founded in 1607 by Captain John Smith); Maryland (chartered by the second Lord Baltimore and founded by his brother, Leonard Calvert in 1634); New York (originally founded as a Dutch colony and taken over by the British in 1664); New Jersey (part of the Dutch colony at New York; given by the British to Lord Berkeley and Sir George Carteret in 1664); Pennsylvania (Quaker settlement founded by William Penn in 1683); Delaware (originally part of Pennsylvania; separated in 1704).

Social Organization

Settlements were founded mainly for economic and religious reasons. They would provide economic opportunity for the inhabitants, and people from different backgrounds and with different religious beliefs would be welcome. Many indentured servants worked four to seven years to pay for their passage to the colonies. Young people learned trades through apprenticeships.

Environment

Longer growing season than in New England with more fertile soil; a greater variety of farms and trades; farming at a greater distance from towns was possible.

Southern Colonies

Carolina (originally founded in 1663; divided into North Carolina and South Carolina in 1729); Georgia (founded as a penal colony by James Oglethorpe in 1733).

Social Organization

Big plantations worked by slaves. Most of the farms were small, however, and did not use slaves. The slave population in the Southern colonies was as large as the population of New England by the 1770s.

Environment

The longest growing season of all, making large plantations profitable; rich, fertile soil conditions prevailed.

✎ ✎ ✎ ✎ ✎

"I see that the computer gave us information about only the British colonies," Babette said. "I know that Spain, France, and Great Britain all colonized America and that the British drove the French out of North America in the French and Indian War. The computer only gave us data about the thirteen original colonies, all of which were established by Great Britain, correct?" Babette was thinking out loud.

"I think so, but that's logical since we asked for information about the American Revolution," Barnaby replied. "What else do we know about the colonies before the Revolution based on this printout?"

Bridget began to pace the floor, preparing to lecture. "Well, it looks like the New England colonies, the Middle colonies, and the Southern colonies were all founded for different reasons. Some people wanted religious freedom, some wanted to make a personal fortune, and some were brought here in chains, against their will."

Beauregard stirred from his catnap long enough to see Bridget delicately stepping over his tail. He had some thoughts of his own about the latter subject, but he would only get angry if he started.

Barnaby now paced the floor with Bridget, only in the opposite direction. "Religious freedom was the most important factor in New England. I can also see the influence of weather and soil conditions on the economic decisions that the colonists made. For instance, New Englanders had to depend more on each other to survive the cold winters and short growing season. They built towns and stuck close to them."

"But they built towns all over the colonies," Bridget replied. "I think it was 'different strokes for different folks' in the Middle colonies. It looks like they were more tolerant, more focused on economic success. The moderate climate and those better soil conditions influenced their thinking. They could live farther apart from each other, if they chose. The only issue I'm not sure about is slavery. Weren't there slaves in Virginia?"

Babette had been following along attentively. "I think so," she said. "Virginia had successful plantations that relied on slave labor. Slavery was attempted throughout the original colonies but it was only profitable in the South, where the long growing season made farming worthwhile."

"That's one thing I'll never understand. How could people sell other people for money?" Bridget said. "I guess greed can drive you to do lots of terrible things, including harm to other people. It harmed African Americans for generations."

Everybody was depressed by the slave thing. It's like finding out that the dark side of the Force is real. Silence filled *Lady Liberty* for a thoughtful moment.

Suddenly, Barnaby spoke up. "So, is it fair to say that all these colonies were developing economically quite well on their own until Great Britain started to tax them?"

"Essentially correct," Beauregard spoke from a reclining position. "Remember that slogan, 'No taxation without representation'? The British had been occupied with fighting wars in Europe, and they left the colonies to govern themselves. When they had to fight the French and Indian War in the American colonies, they decided to make the colonials pay for it. They tried all kinds of taxes to raise money. But they had given the colonials permission to govern themselves and, as it turned out, they had left them alone too long! The colonials were used to governing themselves, to making their own decisions."

"I think we've got data on this taxation issue, too," Barnaby offered. They gathered around to take a look at the printout.

TAXES AND THE
AMERICAN REVOLUTION 1765-1775

The colonists had always considered themselves loyal subjects of Great Britain, but the taxation issue created doubt in their minds. After years of "salutary neglect," the British Parliament had now decided to tax the colonies to pay for Britain's wars, especially those in the colonies known as the French and Indian Wars, which ended in 1763. The colonists objected because they had no elected representatives in the British Parliament. They developed the slogan "No taxation without representation!" to get the message across to the British. Read the following chart as if you were watching a tennis match!

British Tax Law	Colonial Response
Stamp Act, 1765 Colonists must pay taxes on newspapers, legal documents, and licenses.	Colonists riot, claiming the taxes are excessive and unconstitutional.
Quartering Act, 1766 Colonists are responsible for feeding and sheltering British troops.	Colonials claim this is unconstitutional and tyrannical.
Stamp Act Repeal, 1766 Repealed the Stamp Act but claimed that the British Parliament had the same authority in the Americas as it did in Great Britain.	Celebrated the repeal and pledged loyalty to Britain.
Townshend Acts, 1767 Taxes on tea, lead, glass, and newspapers; all but tax on tea repealed.	Rallied the colonists to the slogan, "No taxation without representation;" they boycotted British goods; smugglers profit from tax.
Tea Act, 1773 Reinforced tax on tea and tried to block smugglers.	Boston Tea Party, 342 chests of tea dumped in Boston Harbor.
Intolerable Acts, 1774 Closed Port of Boston and moved troops closer to the city; punished the entire colony.	Armed resistance, beginning in New England and spreading throughout the colonies; colonial legislatures become revolutionary councils.

Bridget sighed, yawned, and stretched. "I could really do without all these facts and dates. They can really put me to sleep."

"Do not think of the facts as something to memorize," Babette suggested. "Try to put the facts together in some useful way, then see if a pattern develops. When you see the pattern, it is easy to remember the facts!"

"Cool! I think I see what you mean. If I see the 'big picture,' I get a better idea of how to put it together. Is that what you mean?" Bridget smiled.

"Excellent," Barnaby interjected. "We've only got a short time to get to St. John's Church, and we don't really know where we are or where we're going. It's time to step outside into 1775! Are we ready?"

"I'd say we are," Bridget replied. "I think we know much more about the reasons for the American Revolution than we did a few hours ago. Let's go!"

The door to the past creaked slowly open as Bridget, Babette, Barnaby, and Beauregard peered cautiously outside. March in Virginia can be a bit tricky to predict, but this particular early evening was warm and breezy. They were full of anticipation about the evening's events, especially now that they knew more about what was going on.

They had landed, oddly enough, in the section of town that later became Monument Avenue. *Lady Liberty* seemed somewhat at home along that magnificent tree-lined street. Wait a minute…Was that a band of gypsies headed down the street right at them? They were all dressed in red and marched in time to the beating of a drum.

"Ah, the redcoats are coming, the redcoats are coming!" Babette cried.

"Do you think they're coming for us?" Bridget asked hesitantly. "They look like a pretty stiff bunch, if you know what I mean. Aren't they the British?"

Without warning, the troops formed a straight line across the street, dropped to one knee, and pointed their muskets directly at the time travelers. "Halt, or we'll shoot!" came the cry from the commanding officer.

Babette leaped into her karate stance and began making all kinds of warning sounds. "Hiyah! Hiyah!" She was chopping the air wildly with her hands in a superb Bruce Lee imitation. The soldiers seemed confused.

The commanding officer approached. "What manner of attack is *that*?" he inquired, somewhat amused. "I say, you realize, of course, that the rules of engagement require you to line up and conduct yourselves properly. None of this kicking and whatnot. How unrefined! Of course, that is the major trouble with you colonials, you are so crude and rude!"

"Well, then, if you don't wish to appear rude, why don't you introduce yourself like a proper officer? As for rules of engagement, we are not looking for a fight, Sir. We have only just arrived here from er, ah, the frontier and we are not familiar with Richmond. Perhaps you can assist us?" Babette's eloquence was remarkable.

"Righto! Captain Horatio Hornblower Bluster at your service! And where might you be headed? Perhaps a costume ball of some sort? I've seen few dressed like you this evening. You'll probably win 'best costume' for that black ensemble, my dear." He turned to Bridget, "And that 'Yank' hat! Are you sure you should be wearing propaganda like that? Actually, I think I'm going to bring you in for questioning under these circumstances. Follow me, please!"

Bridget's frown left no doubt as to how she felt about Captain Bluster. She was not ready to surrender. Beauregard had disappeared, and Barnaby was whispering about outfoxing the British.

Babette and Bridget looked at each other nervously. Captain Bluster and his troops were now marching forward to take them into custody.

"What do we do now?" Bridget said. "It looks like the redcoats mean business."

"I'll see if I can stall them a bit," Barnaby whispered back. "I wonder where Beauregard is?"

Suddenly, there was a blinding flash of light. Barnaby, Babette, and Bridget disappeared from the face of the earth as if someone had beamed them up to a waiting spaceship.

The captain looked bewildered. "My, my, these colonials are truly dreadful. I have tried to be civilized about all this revolutionary rubbish, but I'm running out of patience. Really! Disappearing behind rocks and trees like savages! What is the world coming to? Time for tea!"

Bridget, Babette, and Barnaby found themselves face down on the floor in the main cabin of *Lady Liberty*. They were a little dizzy, but otherwise unharmed.

"Wh—Where are we? Are we back home?" Bridget asked.

"Well, not quite!" a happy Beauregard announced. "But you are safe and sound and out of the reach of the British, for the moment."

"Beauregard, how did you manage to get us aboard?" Barnaby inquired.

"Well, Dr. Tempus had a little secret that I discovered. *Lady Liberty's* torch is a teleportation device. We can materialize anywhere we want, as long as one of us is at the controls."

"Why can't we use the teleporter to get us to St. John's Church before it's too late for Patrick Henry's speech? I wonder where we can get a map of Richmond?" Barnaby asked, scratching his head. He pulled the map from his hair and began looking for the church.

"Here it is, Beauregard!" Barnaby was getting excited about attending his first historical event.

Outside, the torch glowed briefly and three shafts of light shot forth into the city. Beauregard had to make the journey by foot, which gave him an opportunity to learn more about the area.

Some time later, as the large black cat approached St. John's Church, he heard the most famous rallying cry of the American Revolution:

> "I know not what course others may take, but as for me, give me liberty or give me death."

As the crowds left the church, Babette, Bridget, and Barnaby met Beauregard for the walk back to the time machine. They were discussing what they had seen.

"Wow! That guy sure has a way with words! Do you think he's serious? Do you think he'd really rather die than give up his liberty?" Bridget asked thoughtfully.

"Well, he considers the British to be unjust tyrants for imposing all those harsh taxes. It certainly was a long speech, but he was so intense I do not think you could doubt his sincerity," Babette concluded.

"I'm not so sure that everyone in the crowd would agree with you, Babette," Barnaby replied. "Some of them are still loyal to the British crown and think that Henry was preaching treason, an offense punishable by hanging."

"Well, what are we going to do now?" Bridget kicked a loose rock down the cobblestone street. "Are we ready to check out some new scenery or do we want to hang out a while longer in Richmond?"

"Ah ha! I knew I'd find you here among the rabble rousers! Guards, seize them and throw them in the stockade. I'm sure they're colonial spies from the frontier." Captain Bluster just would not disappear!

As the guards prepared to arrest the group, Babette flew—literally—into action. With a high karate kick, she landed one guard squarely in the gut, then rotated in mid-air for another strike at the second guard. Both ended up on their knees. "Yiiieeee hah!" Babette was ready for more, but the guards and the captain had decided to call in re-inforcements, and were rapidly disappearing from view.

"That was cool! You dropped those guys in a second." Bridget was surprised at her own astonishment. Babette, however, appeared unruffled. She smiled back calmly.

Barnaby, equally in awe, said, "That was amazing! But now what do we do? I think we need to get out of this town as fast as we can, before old Captain Bluster seeks revenge. Hey, where's Beauregard? He's disappeared again."

The trio began to look for their friend, then…BANG! It happened again. They found themselves on the floor in *Lady Liberty*.

Beauregard hailed the group with hugs and licks. "I'm getting quite good at this teleportation business, don't you think?"

"Well, three strikes and you're out!" Bridget loved her baseball imagery. "We've already had two close calls with the redcoats and that captain gives me the creeps. I say it's time to beat feet!"

"Where—where are we going next?" Babette said excitedly. How about July 4, 1776, American Independence Day? We would see all of the Founding Fathers like George Washington, Thomas Jefferson, and Ben Franklin.

"That's a great idea!" Barnaby cried. "Are we ready to make the jump? What does that dial Beauregard was talking about read?"

Looking over the instrument panel, Bridget found what looked like a car odometer, only it had dates instead of mileage and in this case was called a "tempometer." "1775," she called back. "Want me to reset the dial?" CLICK.

Everybody froze. The cabin lights flickered wildly and the time-warp hum filled their ears. The last thing any of them heard was Bridget's voice saying, "Here we go again!"

The next thing they heard was an enormously loud THUD! It was followed by another sound, much like a large bell clanging uncontrollably.

Looking out the port hole, Barnaby saw the problem, but could hardly believe his eyes. They had landed directly on top of a church steeple, knocking the bell to the ground. Oddly enough, *Lady Liberty* looked like an excellent replacement for the bell, which now lay in the churchyard, permanently damaged. The "Liberty Bell" would never be rung again!

"There's a man handing out pamphlets down below. Do you think we can move the time machine to the ground without too much fuss?" Bridget inquired.

"I think so. Why don't I aim for that park over there?" Barnaby replied. He navigated the ship without much difficulty and without the city's inhabitants noticing. There was too much going on for anyone to pay much attention to a flying statue.

"Hi, I'm Thomas Paine. Have you read my pamphlet, *Common Sense*? Here, take a look and tell me what you think."

The four friends each took a copy and sat reading it in the nearby park where they had landed *Lady Liberty*. It was July 3, 1776 and they had landed in Philadelphia. What timing!

Beauregard decided to take a nap. It was a warm, lazy afternoon and after all, time travel was stressful, especially when you bumped into people like Captain Bluster.

Babette, Barnaby, and Bridget decided to talk with Mr. Paine about his work. He was still standing on the street discussing his ideas with local citizens. "Mr. Paine," one of the crowd called as Bridget, Barnaby, and Babette walked up, "Why are you so convinced that we need to declare our independence from Great Britain? Don't we stand to lose more than we gain?"

Tom Paine, an Englishman who came to the colonies in November 1774, answered immediately, "Not at all. What we stand to gain is control of our own lives and our own economy. All of you know how we've been taxed unjustly, how we've been forced to buy goods imported from England and the British colonies in the West Indies. Why, they've been taking our raw materials and selling them back to us for more and more profit! I say it's just good common sense for us to take care of our own business—declare independence from a corrupt monarchy and reap the profits of our own hard work. Why should we suffer further injustice at the hands of tyrants?" The crowd applauded loudly.

"Do you think we could meet him?" Babette asked. "I think

he is the man whom George Washington credited with convincing many colonists to fight for independence."

Barnaby was already approaching Mr. Paine. He coughed politely before addressing him. "Hello, Mr. Paine, my name is Barnaby Bain and I'd like you to meet my friends, Bridget and Babette. We heard you speak and we wanted to meet you."

"It is a pleasure to make your acquaintance," Tom Paine replied courteously. "Do you have any questions you'd like to ask me?"

"Yes Sir, I do," Bridget answered. "Some people have said that your pamphlet, *Common Sense*, is just ah…well, er…they say it's just propaganda written to get the colonists to fight for independence. Is that really true?"

"I did publish *Common Sense* to convince the colonists to separate from England for their own benefit. In a sense, I wanted to persuade my readers that we no longer have any good reason to stay loyal to the British monarchy, because they are taking advantage of us both economically and politically. Why should we be taxed on goods shipped to us from England when we can make our own products here? See what I mean? It's just good common sense.

"But maybe that doesn't quite answer your question. Yes, indeed, my arguments are intended to persuade. I don't see any good reasons for us to remain loyal to Great Britain. If you are looking for a balanced argument, however, you are talking to the wrong person! Perhaps you'd like to meet Ben Franklin. He may have some other ideas on the subject. Come, I'll introduce you to him. He's over there in the park, playing with that very large black cat." It seems that Beauregard and Ben had already become acquainted.

Tom Paine introduced Ben Franklin to the group. Ben Franklin is an older man, seventy years of age, with a keen sense of humor and a great deal of wisdom. A printer by trade, Franklin has been an author, a publisher, a scientist, an inventor, and a diplomat in his long, distinguished career.

"I suppose you young people realize that we're getting ready to sign the Declaration of Independence tomorrow," Franklin began. "If you haven't met Thomas Jefferson, I'll introduce you to him later. And I think he might introduce you to some of the ideas he's been developing." He looked up at the gathering thunder-clouds. "Ah, but now it's time for a little experiment!" Ben had a gleam in his eye and an odd little smile on his face. "Let's go fly a kite!" he said suddenly.

Babette and Bridget giggled, and they all marched toward an open, grassy area in the park. Barnaby looked a little uneasy.

"Mr. Franklin, maybe we'd better be careful about being out in open spaces during a thunderstorm. We might be struck by lightning," he ventured.

"Precisely, young Barnaby!" Ben answered, even more excited. "Here, I'm not quite up to running these days. Why don't you get this kite in the air? Hurry, the storm is approaching!"

Bridget, Babette, and Barnaby ran together to get the kite soaring high above the park just as the storm clouds began to simmer. Beauregard, not wanting to get his fur wet, watched the proceedings from beneath a nearby shelter.

Then Ben produced a large key from his pocket. "Now, this is a little experiment about the nature of lightning. We'll thread this key onto the kite string. Keep it close at hand!"

As lightning flashed, Ben had each of the kids touch the key and feel the tingle of electricity. "There. Feel it? This experiment demonstrates that lightning is really electricity. I have always been interested in the nature of electricity, and I enjoy experimenting and publishing the results of my studies. Alas, in my later years, my time has been taken up with political and diplomatic affairs, and my scientific interests have had to take second place. 'God helps those who help themselves' is what I've always said, and so I've spent much of my time negotiating with the British. I'll be heading to France in September to seek their assistance in our struggle with Great Britain."

"Oh, really? I am French," Babette said. "I am sure you will be successful in securing French support."

Ben's face lit up. "You are French? You must meet Thomas Jefferson! He and I have come to know and love many of your countrymen. Mr. Jefferson has learned so much about architecture from the French, not to mention ideas about government."

As twilight fell, Ben invited the foursome home for dinner. The kids and the cat ate ravenously from a feast of fresh summer vegetables, wonderful breads, and roast chicken. After dinner, Ben encouraged them to come with him to visit Thomas Jefferson, the primary author of the Declaration of Independence.

"He's probably still hard at work so we may not want to stay very long," Ben commented.

Sure enough, as they entered Mr. Jefferson's quarters, they found him working by candlelight, quill pen in hand. He stood up to greet them. He was a tall man for his time at six feet, two inches, and his red hair was quite distinctive.

"Thomas, I want you to meet some young friends who have expressed great interest in the Revolution. Tom Paine and I have spent some time with them today and they would like to meet you, too," Ben said.

"Of course, I am happy to meet some of the people to whom I have entrusted the future," Mr. Jefferson said affably. "Would you like to see what I'm writing?"

Ben Franklin shook hands and paws all around and excused himself, leaving the time travelers with Thomas Jefferson as he put the finishing touches on the Declaration of Independence. Beauregard decided to curl up at Jefferson's feet for an after-dinner nap as the conversation began, although he would, of course, keep one furry ear open.

"How does this sound?" Jefferson asked. "See if you think I should change anything." He began to read:

> "We hold these truths to be self-evident, that all men are created equal, that they are endowed by their Creator with certain unalienable Rights, that among these are Life, Liberty and the pursuit of Happiness..."

He finished the reading with a slight smile on his face and looked at his audience. "What do you think? Do you understand what I am saying?"

Bridget spoke first. "I think you mean that all people everywhere have a natural right to lead their own lives and pursue happiness any way they want to. It's sort of like saying that all human beings have a right to be free and that nobody has the right to deny them that. Am I on the right track?"

Jefferson was silent for a moment. "Yes, you are most definitely on the right track! Anybody else have an interpretation?"

Babette spoke next. "I think you also mean that people have the right to free themselves from tyranny. So, if a government is unjust, its citizens have the right to choose a new government. Is that not what you are really doing in this document, claiming that America has a right to be free from tyrannical rule?"

"Yes, that is also an accurate statement. I believe that governments rule because the people give their consent to be governed. The people have a right to change their government whenever they wish. I think, however, that I have also said, 'Eternal vigilance is the price of Liberty.' People might have rights, but they also have responsibilities. So, if we have certain rights, we may choose to exercise those rights only if they do not conflict with other people's freedoms."

"Wait a minute, Mr. Jefferson," Barnaby broke in. "Some people have more ability, more money, more power than others. How could all people be created equal when, in fact, they are born unequal? And another thing, wouldn't the people who have wealth and power have more rights than those who don't?"

"I believe you are touching upon a very important problem, one that will occupy the citizens of this country for generations to come. Even though people may not be *born* equal, they are equal before the law. So, when people's rights conflict, it is not a person's ability or wealth or fame that matters. Conflicts have to be decided based upon the merits of the case. Justice must be blind, so to speak."

Bridget had one more question. "If justice is supposed to be blind, why aren't slaves treated like human beings? Isn't that another problem that all of you are ignoring?"

Thomas Jefferson was visibly disturbed by the question. "I guess you don't realize how much pain the slavery issue has caused all of us. In order to create an independent nation, we have had to make some compromises that are, at best, unfortunate. Some of my countrymen are not willing to sign the Declaration of Independence unless it omits any reference to slavery. I know that it is not right to ignore this problem. We shall have to make some hard decisions when we draft a new constitution for this country."

"How could you *ignore* slavery? It should have been outlawed right from the start," Bridget challenged.

Mr. Jefferson answered only with a look of deep resignation.

"Come on," said Babette, putting her arm around her friend's shoulders. "It is late and everybody is very tired. We all need a good night's sleep. Thank you for your time, Mr. Jefferson. It has been a great honor to meet you."

"Thank you so much for coming, and thank you for your comments," Thomas Jefferson turned to Bridget. "Surely, the honor has been mine."

The group thanked him again and said their good-byes. Thomas Jefferson sat down and took up his quill, ready to continue his work.

On the way back to *Lady Liberty*, the group reflected briefly on the day's events.

"This has been one amazing day," Barnaby said. "We met Thomas Paine, Benjamin Franklin, and Thomas Jefferson and we had quite an interesting discussion about the Declaration of Independence. I guess Americans believe in some very important values, you know, like 'life, liberty, and the pursuit of happiness.'"

"And every generation gets to interpret what those words mean for them," Bridget added.

"Ah, you Americans are so fortunate to have these values written down for all citizens to see and understand! There is nothing quite like it in all the world! This must be one of the reasons why we study history. We *feel* like we belong, like we are a part of something very important. I felt that way today and I am *French!*"

When they awoke the next day, they decided to make another jump, this time to check out General George Washington. The destination? Yorktown, Virginia to see the last battle of the American Revolution.

"Are we ready to jump?" Barnaby called to his friends who were strapping themselves in place. "We're not far from 1781, so this will be a short trip. I'll set the tempometer right now."

The lights flickered, the time warp hummed, then everything fell silent.

"What happened? We didn't go anywhere," Bridget cried.

"Oh yes we did!" Barnaby replied. "Let's look out the porthole."

They crowded around the viewer to catch their first glimpse of the Battle at Yorktown. The battle was fought from September 28, until October 19, 1781, and marked the end of the American Revolution.

"Let's go outside to get a better view," Bridget said.

As they emerged from the hatch of *Lady Liberty*, they could see the French fleet in the Yorktown harbor and the British and American forces engaged in combat.

"Get down! Stay low!" an American infantryman shouted to them. "There's heavy fighting going on. Lord Cornwallis, the British commander, is attempting to break free and escape from Yorktown. He moved here on August 7, and General Washington and the French General Rochambeau pinned him down on land while the French fleet blockaded the harbor. It looks like we've got him!"

Suddenly, a familiar face appeared close to where the time machine had landed. It was none other than Captain Horatio Hornblower Bluster!

"Oh no! Look who's coming! It's Bluster again!" Bridget yelled.

Babette smiled calmly. "Do not worry. We handled him before and we will do it again, if we have to."

"I knew it! I knew it! The second I saw that flying statue of yours come in for a landing, I thought, 'Aye, there's trouble ahead.' I'm here to pay you a little return favor. Prepare to fight!" Captain Bluster exclaimed.

Suddenly, Bluster and his men surrounded the group. There must have been a dozen of them! Barnaby, Bridget, Babette, and Beauregard stood back to back. Badly outnumbered, Babette began to scare the British by chopping wildly at the air with her hands. They backed away a little, but Bluster was ready.

"Seize them!" he cried. "We'll take them as hostages and make Washington and Rochambeau pay a huge ransom to free them! We'll turn the tide of battle with this little victory!"

Without warning, Babette looked at the British troops and yelled, "Hiyaaaaahhhh!" She immediately disabled three redcoats with swift kicks to the stomach. They doubled over on the ground.

"Who is next?" she cried defiantly.

"That will not be necessary, young lady," came a deep voice from a man on horseback. "You've detained them quite admirably and we'll take over from here. You see, you've just stopped the last major attempt by the British to escape the battle. They will have to surrender. There is no escape! I came here to thank you personally for your admirable work."

"Well, who are you?" Bridget demanded.

"Why, excuse me for failing to introduce myself. I am General George Washington, Commander of the Continental Army. I would be most pleased if you would be my guests for the surrender ceremony."

"Ceremony?" Bridget questioned. "Is this a formal occasion?"

"Yes, it is. I will officially accept Lord Cornwallis's surrender and arrange for his withdrawal. The Revolution is over."

The next day, Babette, Bridget, Barnaby, and Beauregard lined up to watch the two armies meet. Representatives from both sides exchanged the terms of surrender, and the British band struck up a tune, "The World Turned Upside Down."

"The colonists rule!" Barnaby thought. "And we were here to see it happen!"

"I wonder what we'll do next?" Bridget thought. "This time travel business is quite an adventure. I think I like it!"

"No wonder I feel so connected to this time and to this place," Babette thought. "The French allies helped to win America its independence."

Beauregard looked at his young friends as they stood lost in thought, and he wondered if any of them had ever enjoyed a better moment in time.

✍ QUIZ #1 ✍
The Colonists Rule!

1. Who said, "Give me liberty or give me death?" Why did he say it?

2. Why did the Pilgrims and the Puritans come to America?

3. Why did colonists settle in the Middle Atlantic and the Southern colonies?

4. What does the slogan "No taxation without representation!" mean?

5. Which British tax law caused the colonists to riot because they considered it excessive and unconstitutional?

6. Which British tax law caused the Boston Tea Party?

7. What series of British laws punished Massachusetts for the Boston Tea Party?

8. Who wrote *Common Sense*? Why did he write it?

9. Which one of the Founding Fathers was known for his experiments with electricity?

10. Who was the primary author of the Declaration of Independence?

✍ FOOD FOR THOUGHT ✍

Here's a good place to start using your journal. Remember, there are lots of possible answers. Be able to say why you think your answer is a good one.

1. Do you think the soil and climate conditions in the colonies had any influence on the continuance of slavery?

2. Suppose you are discussing the American Revolution in class. One of your classmates argues that the American Revolution would never have taken place if the British had not begun to tax the colonists unfairly. Would you agree or disagree with your classmate?

3. What do you think Thomas Jefferson meant by the phrase, "Life, Liberty, and the pursuit of Happiness…"?

4. How did the French influence the outcome of the American Revolution?

5. How do you define propaganda?

✍ GROUP INVESTIGATIONS ✍

Here are some activities that you can do to find out more about the American Revolution. You can do them on your own or with a group. Enjoy yourself!

1. Find out what a typical colonial meal was like and cook one.

2. What did teenagers do for fun in the colonial days? Try out some of their activities for yourself.

3. Who was John Locke? How did his ideas influence Thomas Jefferson?

4. What are the ideals that Americans value most? Which values are most important to you? Why?

5. Stage a skit, draw a picture, write a poem or rap about your life as a colonist.

Chapter 3
Checking Out Some Important Documents

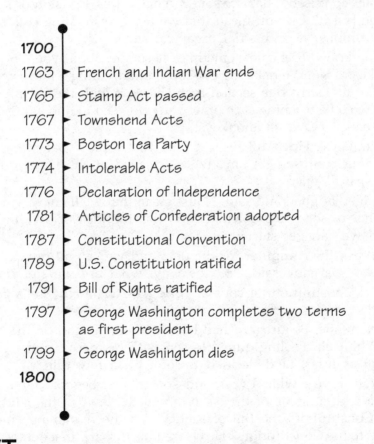

"This is fun," Bridget smiled as they gathered around a circular table to make plans. "I like these little powwows we have from time to time. I sort of enjoy listening to other people's points of view, you know?"

"Yes, I know what you mean," Barnaby replied. "I really enjoyed meeting Ben Franklin and Thomas Jefferson, but I felt like I needed more information. You can ask better questions if you know more about what's going on."

"Exactly, my friends!" Babette chimed in. "And it is even more difficult when you are not born an American! Perhaps we could do a computer search to gather some background information?"

"That's a cool idea, Babette," Bridget said. "Why don't we divide the labor? Barnaby can do some general background and the court system. Babette, you take the president, and I'll take the Congress."

"I am confused," Babette said. "What is this 'division of labor,' as you put it? Do you mean that we are investigating childbirth, labor unions, or industrial organization?"

"You know, Frenchie, sometimes I wonder about you," Bridget chuckled. "No. We're taking one topic and dividing it into sections. Each of us learns one section then shares it with the group. That way, we'll be teaching each other stuff we need to know! It's more fun than a barrel of monkeys!"

"Monkeys? How did we get onto that topic?" Babette asked, sounding confused. "I am always amazed at the way you say things, Bridget!"

Bridget laughed and said, "I just mean that we'll enjoy working together to solve a problem. If you like the idea of dividing the labor, we can get started."

"I'll ask the computer for the data and we can all prepare our reports," Barnaby said. "By the way, what are we studying?"

"The Constitution, of course!" Bridget exclaimed. "Let's get to work!"

Meanwhile, Beauregard had been playing around on the computer himself. Feeling quite pleased with his new-found technological abilities, he'd decided to look up a few things.

"Well, here's what I've found so far," he began. "First, let's take a look at some of the basics about the laws of the land, the U.S. Constitution, the Bill of Rights, and the remaining amendments to the Constitution." He cleared his throat. "In a democracy, the people make rules to govern themselves, and the Preamble (that is, the introduction) to the Constitution, makes it quite clear that the people of the United States rule!

WE THE PEOPLE of the United States, in Order to form a more perfect Union, establish justice, insure domestic Tranquility, provide for the common defence, promote the general Welfare, and secure the Blessings of liberty to ourselves and our Posterity, do ordain and establish this CONSTITUTION for the United States of America.

"The Preamble sets the stage for the establishment of the federal government and spells out the relationship between the federal government and the state governments. Each of the seven articles in the U.S. Constitution has a special purpose. We need to keep in mind, however, that citizens in a democracy have a big responsibility, they must stay awake and participate! The Constitution tells us the way the government is supposed to work and what our rights and responsibilities are as citizens of the United States." Beauregard sat down importantly. He was still feeling pleased with himself and wondered if he'd be able to play around on the computer again later.

Barnaby had been busy at the computer himself during Beauregard's contribution. "Hey, listen to this," he said. "Something unexpected just popped up. Did you know that the Constitution was not the first national governmental framework? In 1781, after the British defeat at Yorktown, there was no national government until the Articles of Confederation were adopted as the law of the land. It didn't work very well. A confederacy means that the national government is weak and the individual state governments are strong. The states were always squabbling among themselves and the national government was too weak to settle the disputes. By 1787, it was obvious that the Articles of Confederation had to be replaced, and quickly!

"So, fifty-five delegates met in Philadelphia during the summer of 1787 and drafted the U.S. Constitution. George Washington presided over the meeting, lending his leadership and prestige to the proceedings. All the big names were there—I guess it was sort of like Oscars night in Hollywood. Franklin, Adams, Madison, Jefferson. James Madison of Virginia is often called the "Father of the Constitution" because he was a constitutional scholar and a staunch defender of the document once it was established. He kept careful notes of the discussion throughout the 1787 convention and these were eventually published for everybody to read.

Alexander Hamilton, John Jay, and James Madison wrote *The Federalist*, a famous book containing eighty-five papers that defended the Constitution from attack around the country. The Constitution was ratified by a two-thirds majority of the states by March 4, 1789 and became the official governing document.

The Bill of Rights, the first ten amendments (changes) to the Constitution were added in 1791, after they were ratified by the states.

"Wow! And don't you think it's kind of cool to think that the Constitution is about seven thousand words long and has lasted over two hundred years?"

"It sure is," Bridget agreed. "Okay, listen up, because I've found some information on the Congress."

Article I: The Congress

Congress consists of two houses, the House of Representatives and the Senate. The two houses make Congress what's called a bicameral legislature. The House of Representatives members serve two-year terms and the number of representatives is based on population. James Madison came up with this idea and it was called the 'Virginia Plan.' Members of the Senate are elected to six-year terms and each state gets two senators regardless of the size of the state or the population. That way, big states with more people don't have more power than small states with fewer people. This idea for the Senate was called the 'New Jersey Plan' because it was proposed by the New Jersey delegation. This business of having two houses in the legislature was called the Great Compromise because it satisfied those who favored the Virginia Plan as well as those who favored the New Jersey Plan. Just remember that Congress is the national legislature and makes laws for the whole country. So, Article I of the Constitution is all about Congress and the powers of Congress. Babette, what have you got on Article II?"

Article II: The President

"Article II is very interesting! American presidents and their powers really interest people all around the world. It is ironic that this person is one of the most powerful people on the planet but also one of the weakest. Or maybe it is checks and balances I am thinking about...

"American presidents enjoy a wide range of powers but they are limited by a system of checks and balances among the three branches of government. While Congress makes laws, the president frequently proposes a legislative agenda. In fact, the success or failure of his administration may depend on how much of his agenda he can persuade Congress and the American people to support. Essentially, his power is the power to persuade. His constitutional duties include being commander-in-chief of the armed forces, appointing judges to federal courts including the Supreme Court, developing American foreign policy, and creating a budget for the federal government. The president is the head of the executive branch and it is his responsibility to make sure that the laws that Congress enacts are put into action unless, of course, he vetoes the legislation and sends it back to Congress. That is one of those checks and balances I mentioned earlier. Anyway, the president is an important leader whom people often regard as a symbol of the country. His term of office is four years and, since the adoption of the twenty-second amendment, he may be reelected only once.

"Do you not think it is interesting to see how all this works on a daily basis? If you watch the news or read the newspaper, for example, you can see that the president, the Congress, and the Supreme Court agree to disagree on many important issues. Barnaby, what have you found out about Article III?"

Article III: The Judiciary

"Article III is about the judicial branch and how it is organized," Barnaby began. "When you think of the judiciary, think judges and courts. The Constitution provides for a system of federal courts that handles cases involving federal laws. There are federal district courts, federal courts of appeal, and finally, the Supreme Court. Although the Constitution doesn't really say so, the Supreme Court interpreted the Constitution to say that it had the right of 'judicial review.' This means that the Supreme Court has the right to judge the constitutionality of legislation. If it declares a law unconstitutional, that law becomes null and void. Whether it's a state or federal law, it's trashed! The Supreme Court can also reverse decisions of the lower courts and hear cases involving disputes between states. It can also refuse to hear cases and let lower court decisions stand. Federal judges are appointed by the president with the approval of Congress.

"Okay, now that we've looked at the three branches of government established by the Constitution, what are we left with? Let's take a look at these."

Barnaby picked up a bunch of papers from the printer that gave brief statements about the remaining articles, that is, IV-VII. Here's what they said:

> **Article IV: How states relate to each other and to the federal government**
> Article IV establishes the way the federal government and the states are going to deal with each other. Its purpose is to avoid misunderstandings about the way things are supposed to be accomplished.
> **Article V: Amending the Constitution**
> Unlike the Articles of Confederation which stated that all the states had to agree to a change, the Constitution can be amended when Congress, the president, and three-quarters of the state legislatures approve of a change. Two-thirds of the state legislatures can also initiate an amendment to the Constitution.
> **Article VI: The Constitution is the supreme law of the land**
> When laws conflict with the Constitution, the Constitution takes precedence over any other law.
> **Article VII: Ratification**
> Article VII establishes a process for approving changes to the Constitution.

"Excellent!" said Beauregard. "Now let's move on to the Bill of Rights." He picked up his papers importantly. "You might have noticed," he began, "that the Bill of Rights, which also happens to be the first ten amendments to the Constitution, came two years after the Constitution became the law of the land. There was quite a debate about the tyranny that a strong central government could inflict on the people unless individual liberties were guaranteed under the Constitution. So, the Bill of Rights sets out a series of individual liberties that every American citizen possesses. The only problem is that these rights often conflict with each other. But let's take a look at them before we get into that:

The Bill of Rights

First Amendment: Freedom of religion; freedom of speech; freedom of the press; freedom of assembly and petition

Second Amendment: The right to bear arms

Third Amendment: Quartering of soldiers limited

Fourth Amendment: Prohibition against unlawful searches and seizures

Fifth Amendment: Right to due process of law; protection against self-incrimination

Sixth Amendment: The rights of a person accused of a crime, including the right to legal representation

Seventh Amendment: The right to a trial by jury

Eighth Amendment: Unfair bail, fines, and punishment forbidden

Ninth Amendment: Citizens entitled to the rights not listed in the Constitution

Tenth Amendment: Powers not listed reserved to the states or the people"

"See, I told you, Barnaby!" Bridget said. "All these amendments protect the rights of the average citizen. I guess those guys really thought that power could be abused and that innocent people might suffer if the wrong people got elected to office."

"I guess you're right, Bridget. And I guess the Founding Fathers learned from experience, because they had to fight a tyrant for *their* freedom in the first place. That must have been one of the reasons why they felt so strongly about protecting the individual rights of citizens. I mean, Jefferson and the Virginia delegation wouldn't ratify the Constitution until they were guaranteed a Bill of Rights!"

"That's so cool," said Bridget.

"Ah, yes it is, Bridget," Babette began. "Americans often forget how unique the Bill of Rights is. In America, a person accused of a crime is innocent until proven guilty. But in much of the world, it is the other way around—an accused person is guilty until proven innocent. That is wonderful protection from illegal arrest and imprisonment."

"Yeah, Babette, you're right," Bridget said. "And I'll tell you something else, 'You snooze, you lose!' If you don't know your rights, you're missing out. If you're not able to afford an attorney and you're accused of a crime, the court will appoint an attorney for you free of charge. Your home is protected from illegal searches. You don't have to testify against yourself. And all this on top of the freedom of religion, of speech, and of the press. I guess I hadn't really thought about the advantages of being an American citizen."

"But we shouldn't start waving flags yet, Bridget. I mean, lots of problems can develop because these rights have limits. For example, while I might have freedom of speech, that doesn't give me the right to defame somebody's character. Citizens need to know their rights, but they also need to respect the rights of others," Barnaby cautioned.

"Oh, Barnaby! I wish you didn't have to play Captain Bringdown all the time! Anyway, now I want to take a look at these other amendments. Mind if we proceed? Here's a copy of the printout for you and Babette."

Eleventh Amendment (1798): Rules for lawsuits against states adopted

Twelfth Amendment (1804): New rules for electing the president and vice president

Thirteenth Amendment (1865): Abolition of slavery

Fourteenth Amendment (1868): Rights of citizenship, due process, and equal protection under the law

Fifteenth Amendment (1870): Voting rights for former slaves

Sixteenth Amendment (1913): Federal income tax

Seventeenth Amendment (1913): Direct election of U.S. senators

Eighteenth Amendment (1919): Prohibition—alcohol banned

Nineteenth Amendment (1920): Women's right to vote

Twentieth Amendment (1933): Presidential and congressional terms in office set

Twenty-first Amendment (1933): Repeal of Prohibition

Twenty-second Amendment (1951): President limited to two terms

Twenty-third Amendment (1961): District of Columbia gains right to vote

Twenty-fourth Amendment (1964): No poll taxes

Twenty-fifth Amendment (1967): Presidential succession and disability

Twenty-sixth Amendment (1971): Voting age lowered to eighteen

Twenty-seventh Amendment (1992): Congressional salaries regulated

"Well, I think we've now got all the basics on the Constitution together," said Beauregard. "That makes us about ready for our next jump."

✍ QUIZ #2 ✍
Checking Out Some Important Documents

1. What are the first ten amendments to the U.S. Constitution called?

2. What was the first national government of the U.S. called?

3. Who is referred to as the "Father of the Constitution"?

4. What is a legislature called if it has two houses?

5. Which branch of the federal government makes law?

6. Which branch of the federal government makes sure that legislation is enacted?

7. What branch of the federal government deals with courts and judges?

8. What is the Supreme Court's ability to judge the constitutionality of legislation called?

9. Which amendment guarantees freedom of religion, speech, and press as well as the right to assembly and petition?

10. Who is responsible for developing American foreign policy?

✐ FOOD FOR THOUGHT ✐

If you are using a journal, continue to write or draw your responses to any of the following questions that interest you. Be able to say why you think your answer is a good one.

1. Why do you think that some of the founding fathers were so insistent on drawing up a Bill of Rights?

2. Pick out a controversy that you've read, heard about or discussed in the last few months. What is your position on the issue? Gather evidence to support your position, then gather information about the opposite point of view. What rights are in conflict? Which amendments to the Constitution are involved? How would you solve the problem?

3. Whenever the Constitution is studied, people talk about a system of "checks and balances." What are they talking about? Why do we have checks and balances?

4. Here's a new piece of information! The Three Fifths Compromise said that slaves were to count as three fifths of a person when determining the population of a state for representation. Why didn't the founding fathers outlaw slavery? How would you have solved the issue?

5. Why has the U.S. Constitution remained such a flexible document?

Chapter 4
Exploring the New Frontier

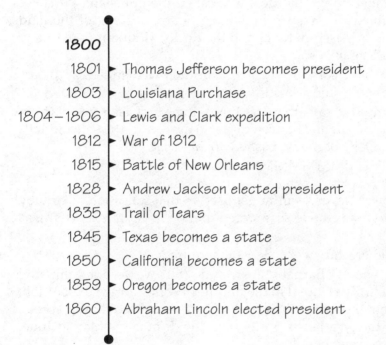

1800

1801	Thomas Jefferson becomes president
1803	Louisiana Purchase
1804–1806	Lewis and Clark expedition
1812	War of 1812
1815	Battle of New Orleans
1828	Andrew Jackson elected president
1835	Trail of Tears
1845	Texas becomes a state
1850	California becomes a state
1859	Oregon becomes a state
1860	Abraham Lincoln elected president

"Is it time? Are we ready?" Bridget was ready to set forth on another adventure. "I'm getting kind of tired of sitting around like this. Let's go and meet some pioneering types. Don't you think they would be fun?"

"Dangerous, too, I bet!" Barnaby was feeling cautious after their recent encounters with the British. "I think it would be interesting to meet some Native Americans. Why don't we head for the frontier?"

"That sounds wonderful," Babette said enthusiastically. "Just one thing. How do we know when we have reached the frontier? Surely it would depend on what year we pick?"

"Yeah, I guess you're right," Bridget said. "The frontier changed as the country expanded. So which one do we want to see?"

"The United States bought some land from France, yes? I remember something about Emperor Napoleon selling a large parcel of land for fifteen million dollars and it included the city of New Orleans. 'A good deal,' as you Americans would say. Maybe we should explore that territory," Babette said.

"I remember now! That deal was called the Louisiana Purchase and it doubled the size of the United States, adding all the land between the Mississippi River and the Rocky Mountains." Barnaby was excited again.

"Okay, what year do we pick?" Bridget demanded. "I mean, I really have to know a little more about where I'm going!"

"The computer says that the Louisiana Purchase took place in 1803 when President Thomas Jefferson agreed to the sale. So let's head for 1804!" Barnaby rushed to his seat.

CLICK! HUMMMMMMMMM…

"Wow! I never seem to get used to that sensation," Barnaby muttered to himself. He scampered to the viewer to see what was outside.

"Well, where are we?" Babette inquired.

"I don't know," Barnaby answered, "but we've got company! It looks like we've landed in the middle of some kind of expedition, judging from the size of their packs. They're dressed like explorers. Looks like the weather is pretty nice, too. It must be May or June. Let's go and say hello!"

Babette, Barnaby, Bridget, and Beauregard emerged from the cabin of *Lady Liberty* into a new world, an unspoiled environment where the air, water, and vegetation were pure and clean. They all took deep breaths, savoring the taste of a beautiful summer's day.

"Did President Jefferson send you? I've never seen such an unusual vehicle! I'm Meriwether Lewis and this is my associate William Clark. We're exploring the Louisiana territory and looking for a northwest passage through the wilderness all the way to the Pacific Ocean. What news do you bring us?" Lewis and Clark were obviously very excited by the group's arrival.

"Uh uh...keep up the good work!" Bridget responded glibly. "Actually, we're explorers, too, and we were hoping to catch a glimpse of life on the frontier when we found you guys. We really don't have any message from President Jefferson."

Lewis and Clark looked hard at the kids and the cat, then at each other, eyebrows raised. "Sorry, but this is not an easy trip," Clark began. "Many of our men are privates in the army. They trained for several months in order to prepare themselves for a long and difficult journey. After all, until now no one has explored the continent all the way to the Pacific Ocean."

"Actually, we do not wish to travel with you," Babette responded. "We would just like to look around a little. We promise we will not get in your way."

The two explorers hesitated for a moment, a look of concern crossing their faces. "Well, okay, but just stay out of trouble," Meriwether Lewis replied. "We're getting ready to break camp. We're keeping detailed journals for President Jefferson so that he can learn as much as possible about the new territory. I'll tell you what, why don't you explore the area around our camp and make observations?"

"That sounds kind of interesting. Should we be aware of anything in particular?" Bridget asked.

"Well, now that you mention it, Mr. Jefferson left us very detailed instructions," Lewis said, suddenly perking up. "He wants us to observe Native American tribal customs, trade opportunities, plant and animal life, geography, mineral deposits, and weather conditions. He also wants us to make observations about the number of rainy, cloudy, and clear days and about the amount of snow, rain, hail, and frost." Lewis held up his observation journal enthusiastically. He obviously loved exploring and his enthusiasm was not lost on the time travelers.

"Of course we'll help with the observations!" Barnaby announced. "I've completed several climate, and soil analyses and I'm sure my friends would like to assist me."

"Where do we start?" Babette wondered aloud. "There is so

much wilderness. It is so primitive, so untamed. Do you think you would be able to send someone along with us to show us around?"

William Clark responded quickly. "Why don't I send my slave, York, to walk around with you?"

"Slave?" Bridget asked stiffly. "You own a slave?"

Clark seemed uneasy. "Yes, I do, but I intend to give him his freedom when we return from this expedition. Right now, we're extremely fortunate to have the benefit of his talents. He understands many Native American customs and is a highly skilled hunter."

Bridget fidgeted, but this Lewis looked like a nice sort of guy, so she decided he probably would give York his freedom when the expedition was over. She decided not to pursue it.

So Bridget, Babette, and Barnaby started to walk around the area surrounding the camp with York. He began to tell them about all the provisions that the explorers had brought along. "We have several thousand pounds of pork, salt, flour, and biscuits for the trip. Everyone seems to think we're going to find a water route to the Pacific Ocean, so we're traveling rivers like the Missouri as far as we can. The search for the Northwest Passage is one of the reasons why we're making this trip."

"Fascinating," Barnaby responded. "I had no idea that you traveled so far by boat and that you had so much food. Don't you get tired of eating the same old thing every day?"

"Sometimes. But we also hunt for all kinds of wild game and fish the streams to supplement what we brought with us. We keep journals to document the types of game and the numbers we see." York was carefully walking the group around the perimeter of the base camp. That way, they could observe the activities of the explorers while also looking at the lush forest landscape.

Suddenly, York dropped to one knee and pointed into the trees near the camp. "Look!" he said with hushed excitement. "We're being stalked by a cougar! I guess he thinks one of us might make a good meal!"

"Cougar?" Bridget inquired. "Where, where? I don't think I've ever seen one before."

Everybody was squinting in an effort to see the feline predator that was stalking them. Finally, Babette spotted the animal as it crouched in the trees above their heads.

Suddenly, Bridget let out a yelp. York had pointed his musket directly at the cougar and was preparing to fire! She grabbed the muzzle of the musket, causing York to miss his target and fire into the air.

"Why did you do that?" York yelled. "That animal's fur is worth a fortune! Besides, he's a threat to our safety."

"Hold on just a minute there, Mr. York, or whatever your name is," Bridget snapped. "That cat you're aiming at is neither fur nor foe. In fact, he's a personal friend of ours and we'd all prefer you to aim at something else, if you don't mind! Beauregard, get down out of that tree before York makes a pelt out of you!" she shouted at the forest above their heads.

Beauregard had been resting in the treetop, enjoying the fresh air and keeping a watchful eye on his friends and the camp below. However, in this heat, it seems he had closed his eyes for a moment. He scurried down the tree, almost fell at the bottom, but regained his composure and walked with an air of defiance toward the group.

"Whew! That was a close call!" Barnaby said nervously. "We'd be lost without Beauregard. Maybe he should hang out with us while we're visiting the Louisiana territory, just so he's not mistaken for wild game by anybody else."

Babette noticed Beauregard's whiskers twitching and decided it was best to change the subject. "So, this is the pioneer experience I have heard Americans talk about! Speaking of survival skills, every day out here in the wilderness must be a struggle. Do you spend much of one day preparing for the next?" she asked York.

"Absolutely," York responded, looking straight at Babette, and not at Beauregard. "Our survival skills include knowing how to hunt, fish, and trap as well as construct homes and furniture, and make clothing. We also have to know how and what to cook. We need discipline to survive. Why, we'll have to winter in several places along the way once it's too cold to travel."

It didn't work. Beauregard was still twitching. He was more than a little annoyed at all the fur and pelt talk he had overheard. "I must say, I feel a certain sense of disgust that animals' furs are sold for economic gain. Is it *really* necessary?" he asked pointedly.

York was surprised to find Beauregard so articulate but he

understood the question only too well. "I guess I must answer 'yes' to your question, Beauregard," he replied, turning to the large black cat. "I apologize for almost shooting you but the value of fur, especially to pioneers and Native Americans, is not just a matter of money. I know only too well that greed is always a motivation for some people, but people on the frontier buy and sell furs for economic and physical survival, not because they're cruel. Yes, I definitely understand your question," he added. "Can you imagine being bought and sold on an auction block as I was?"

"Well, because I am a rather sophisticated cat, I understand why the pioneers and the Native Americans need animals for their survival. Just don't expect me to like it!" Beauregard responded. His whiskers had finally stopped twitching, which he was relieved about, even though the others had pretended not to notice.

By this time, York had led the group around the entire camp and they were standing on the banks of the wild Missouri River. Lewis and Clark rejoined them after the tour.

"Won't you join us for dinner?" Lewis offered. "We've got a good supply of food that you're welcome to share with us."

Beauregard began to look much happier. "Food? Now there's a good idea," he thought. "Yes, I could do with a little something," he replied. "I'd be happy to help with the preparation, if you like."

"I've never met a feline chef before but sure, go ahead. Maybe you can give the cook a few lessons!" Lewis chuckled.

As they sat around the campfire at twilight, the group savored the joys of a wonderful meal and talked about the expedition.

"I am curious about the Native Americans and their languages and customs," Babette said. "Do you have much trouble communicating with them?"

"We have York, who is good at communicating with Native Americans, but actually, we're hoping to find a French Canadian fur trader who has been living in this territory. He would be useful as a guide and a translator," William Clark said. "We hear that there are some very large mountains that we have to cross and we'll need help to find a way through. Do you have any suggestions?"

"You might find that a Native American woman by the name

of Sacajawea would be the perfect person to help you," Bridget interjected. "I remember her name from history class! It means 'Bird Woman' and she's married to a French Canadian guy and they have a baby, too."

Suddenly, a very startled look crossed Bridget's face and she stopped talking abruptly. "Oops! I think you should forget what I just said," she squeaked.

"How do you know about such a woman?" Meriwether Lewis asked, his eyes carefully watching Bridget's reaction.

"Well...er...a...just a hunch, I guess," Bridget said sheepishly. "Don't you think we should be hitting the sack soon? I mean, we've taken up so much of your time already. Thanks for a wonderful dinner." Bridget was backing away from the campfire toward *Lady Liberty*.

Meriwether stood up. "Wait a minute! How did you know about the Native American woman? Where are you from? Are you spies? British spies out to sabotage our efforts? I think we'd better detain them for questioning," he said sternly.

Without warning, *Lady Liberty*'s warp drive began a low-pitched hum. Somebody was back in the main cabin! Beauregard!

Bridget, Babette, and Barnaby were in a full run with the Lewis and Clark expedition right behind them. As they slammed the door shut just ahead of the pursuing mob, Beauregard ordered, "Prepare for immediate launch! We've got to get out of here before they decide to start shooting and damage the ship!"

CLICK! The low drone turned high pitched, the lights began flashing, and suddenly Meriwether Lewis and William Clark were staring into thin air. Bewildered, they returned to their camp wondering who their strange visitors had really been. When they met Sacajawea and her French Canadian husband, Toussaint Charbonneau and their infant son Jean-Baptiste that winter, they decided it was best not to record the arrival of three kids and a talking cat in their observation journal. "Let's just forget all about it," Lewis had said.

It was another quick jaunt. When the lights returned to normal Bridget, Babette, Barnaby, and Beauregard sat silently for a moment, contemplating their top-speed arrival at yet another time in history. It really was quite incredible.

"That was a close call, in more ways than one!" Barnaby said. "We must remember that we can alter the present if we tamper with the past. Remember, Dr. Tempus Fugit warned us about that problem!"

"Oh, stop being so preachy, Barnaby," Bridget replied. "I made a mistake, okay? I'll try to be more careful. Hey, where are we anyway? Anybody checked out the year?"

"It looks as though we made a ten-year jump to 1814," Barnaby said. "And we've changed locations. I can see mountains and rolling hills. I think we've gone east, judging from the terrain."

"We will be able to get a better idea of our position in the morning," Babette reasoned. "I think we should all get some sleep right now. I am exhausted after that last encounter."

They awoke early the next morning to the sound of drums—angry, threatening drums. They peeked out of the viewer at the morning landscape, but that wasn't all…they were surrounded by Native American warriors, who didn't look happy.

"What'll we do now?" Bridget asked nervously. "Those guys look like they really mean business!"

"I'll go out and speak with them," Babette replied matter-of-factly.

"Whoa, Frenchie!" Bridget cried. "You aren't going out there by yourself. Beauregard can stay on board while the rest of us try to show our peaceful intentions. That way, we can still run if we get in a jam."

Bridget, Babette, and Barnaby popped the hatch and exited the time machine with weird-looking smiles plastered on their faces. As soon as they stepped out, they were surrounded by Native Americans.

The chief approached. Babette began to gesture. She was using universal sign language! Bridget and Barnaby were amazed.

"The chief wants to know what we are doing here," Babette whispered to her friends. "What shall I say?"

"Tell him that we come in peace to explore the territory," Barnaby suggested. Babette signed the message.

The chief suddenly got very agitated. "That is what all white people say! Then they try to take our land from us by settling here without our permission," Babette translated. "He wants us to come with him to his village. I do not think we have much choice. I hope Beauregard is watching!"

They walked through the forest to a clearing where the Native Americans had built their village. The smell of campfires filled the air as the warriors brought the trio into a central clearing. Babette signed a question to the chief, who was still looking stern and unhappy.

"What do you want with us?" she asked. "We really are not interested in settling on your land. In fact, we will leave now, if you wish."

The chief nodded and Bridget, Babette, and Barnaby were led to the center of the clearing and tied to a large stake.

"Now you are my hostages and I will bargain with the white people for your release! That should convince them to leave our land and our people alone," the chief signed.

Babette sighed. She was ready to demonstrate her black belt skills but she knew the odds were against her—there were just too many of them, and they had spears. She looked at her companions and said, "I think we better wait for Beauregard. I have a feeling he will be here soon."

She had just finished speaking when Beauregard appeared on the edge of the clearing. He cut quite a dashing figure, his sleek black coat against the green trees behind him. Turning to follow the kids' eyes, the chief was clearly impressed.

He signed to the group, "Is that cougar a personal friend of yours? I have never seen one walk on his hind legs like that!"

"He is a special friend of ours who has many talents," Babette signed back. "His spirit is loyal to us and he has been our guardian through many learning experiences."

"You speak of your friend's spirit with respect. Those who are friends of the cougar are our friends also," the chief responded. "We are not, after all, uncivilized people."

Babette, Bridget, and Barnaby suddenly found themselves free of restraints. Beauregard reached the group and addressed the chief and his warriors. "You show my spirit great respect by releasing my friends. We will withdraw from your land if you will kindly direct us toward the white people's settlement." Babette signed the message as Beauregard spoke.

The chief was even more impressed. He bowed graciously to Beauregard and the group and offered them refreshments before they left.

The time travelers and the chief exchanged farewells, and the chief directed them toward the settlement. "My warriors will escort you as far as they can, but you must know that we are not on good terms with the white people. You must be very careful," he warned.

"Looks like we landed in the middle of some kind of war," Bridget said, as they walked toward the settlement. "Do we know anything about what's happening out here?"

"I took the liberty of checking the computer before I left the ship," Beauregard replied. "We are in the middle of the 1812 war! It seems the British and Americans started fighting again over control of the high seas. The Creek Indians were allies of the British this time, thinking they would regain the hunting grounds they had lost to the American settlers. One Shawnee tribal chief, Tecumseh, was particularly influential in getting Native Americans to attack American settlements throughout the Louisiana territory. But Tecumseh was killed and General Andrew Jackson became famous after he defeated the Creeks and made them give up much of their land. General Jackson also defeated the British at the Battle of New Orleans in 1815, even though the British and the Americans had already signed a peace treaty. General Jackson became a great war hero because he defeated both the Native Americans and the

British in the 1812 war. He became president of the United States in 1828. President Jackson eventually forced all the Native Americans living east of the Mississippi River to abandon their homes and farms and move to the Oklahoma territory. Many Native Americans became sick and died along the way. Their difficult journey was called the Trail of Tears."

Bridget spoke first. "I never knew that Native Americans suffered so much during the early years. Thanks for filling us in, Beauregard. I feel like I know where I am, sort of. I mean…well, I have an idea about what's happening out here. I was clueless until now!"

"I know what you mean, Bridget." Barnaby was reflecting on their recent experiences. "I'd like to meet Andrew Jackson just to see what he's really like. He's quite an important character."

"I once read that he was the first president elected by the common people—a 'people's president' was the phrase I remember," Bridget said.

"I would like to meet Andrew Jackson, too," Babette agreed. "He also sounds like a kind of pioneer."

Their Native American guides indicated to Babette that they could proceed no further, so the foursome raised their hands and paws in the universal peace sign and parted company with their Creek friends. It had been quite a morning.

The time travelers headed into the settlement where they began to inquire about the general's whereabouts. The locals told them that they were in the middle of Tennessee territory near Nashville and that the general was out fighting the Native Americans, so they would have a difficult time catching up with him.

"What should we do?" Bridget asked. "Perhaps we should take a trip to 1828 to see if we can visit him when he's president. That would be cool."

There was a chorus of agreement from the group, and they headed off toward *Lady Liberty*. Somehow, this option seemed a little less dangerous. When they arrived, Barnaby set the tempometer for 1828. The trip took a little longer this time, but they made the jump without a hitch.

"**W**ow! Take a look at that crowd of people out there," Barnaby said as he looked through the viewer. "They appear to be headed for a celebration of some sort. What could it be?" He continued looking at the surroundings, then exclaimed, "Hey! We're in Washington, D.C.! I can see the White House and everybody is headed for the lawn."

"Come on, let's see what all the commotion is about," Bridget suggested. So Bridget, Barnaby, Babette, and Beauregard joined the throng heading toward the White House lawn.

"Look at that," Barnaby said. He was pointing at a large group of people who were getting a little unruly as they surrounded a table holding what looked like a huge wheel of cheese. "They're fighting over the cheese," he said in amazement. "I think we'd better get out of here before they start to riot."

Too late. The crowd began to eddy like leaves caught in a dirt devil on a dry summer's day. It looked like the White House was under siege by the common people.

"What's going on?" Bridget asked a passerby. "What's everybody so excited about?"

"Why, where have you been for the past six months? Andrew Jackson's inauguration was today and he invited the whole country to attend. They've opened up the White House and there's supposed to be plenty of food and drink for everyone! Trouble is, people have gotten kind of rowdy and there aren't enough police to keep the peace. If I were you young folk, I'd head on out of this area before you get caught up in the madness!"

"How are we going to get to meet Andrew Jackson on this important day?" Bridget thought to herself. Then, she said, "Hey, I've got an idea. Let's see if we can sneak in through a side entrance. In all this commotion, we might just be able to walk right into his office!"

The kids and the cat headed down the side of the building and, sure enough, there was another entrance. They walked right into the White House!

It didn't take them long to spot a tall, white-haired man talking to a group of people. The man said, "I believe that everybody has a part to play in a democratic government. Before me, most presidents came from wealthy backgrounds. Well, I'm going to change all that. The common people will be asked to serve in this administration, not just the wealthy. In fact, I'm a kind of pioneer myself, being the first president born west of the Appalachian Mountains. I don't trust the wealthy or the educated to rule. This government must include people from all classes, educated and uneducated!"

"That is President Jackson!" Babette whispered to Barnaby. "He is really quite a distinguished looking man, but he is not like Jefferson or Franklin. He is proud of his pioneer background and suspicious of educated people. He wants everyday people to be part of his government. I wonder why?"

"Let's see if we can get close enough to ask him a question," Barnaby whispered back. "Maybe he'll tell us why."

Bridget, Barnaby, Babette, and Beauregard inched their way closer to the man at the center of the group. Barnaby raised his hand to attract the president's attention.

"Yes, son." President Jackson pointed his long index finger directly at Barnaby, and the latter jumped when the president's steely glare met his eyes.

"I wonder if I might ask you a question, Sir," Barnaby began respectfully. The president nodded. "I hear you say that the wealthy and the educated are not the only people fit for government service, but why should uneducated people rule?"

There was a stunned silence, as if someone had said something inappropriate.

"Why, son, I'll repeat myself if I have to, but I thought I made it clear that in a democracy the common people are the ones who should run the government, not the wealthy few or the educated elite. Look around you! All these people are here to celebrate the triumph of the common man, who I represent! I'll see to it that everyday people have a part to play in their government. Now, does that answer your question?"

Barnaby shrugged. "Yes, Mr. President, it does, but I'm still confused about uneducated people. How do people who are not educated make good decisions?"

The president's face reddened, and he seemed a little flustered when he responded. "Don't you trust common people to make good decisions, young man?" he began. "There are lots of things I don't know or understand but I know that I'll make the right decisions, despite what some upper-class types might think. Maybe you ought to think about that a little."

"Thank you, Mr. President," Barnaby replied politely. He was still not sure what to think of President Jackson's response.

"I think I've had enough for one day!" Barnaby said quietly, turning to his friends. "Let's head back to the ship for a meal and a rest."

The foursome left the White House and were heading toward *Lady Liberty* when they overheard two men talking.

"You know, one day this country is going to spread from the Atlantic to the Pacific. We may have to fight, but we're destined to rule. It couldn't be more obvious!"

"You're right, Mr. Polk. One day this great country will spread from sea to shining sea. Right now, we have to work to make that vision a reality, don't you think?"

"I agree wholeheartedly, Sir. I must convince President Jackson that I am the man who should one day fill his shoes," James K. Polk replied.

Bridget nudged Barnaby in the ribs and whispered, "Hey, that guy's going to be president one day! I can't believe that we saw him, too! He's the one that believes in manifest destiny, you know, the country's got to reach the Pacific no matter who or what's in the way. Sort of makes me wonder if these guys really believed in the common people."

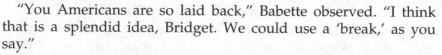

As they reached the time machine, the foursome decided they could afford to spend the evening relaxing. Beauregard started meal preparations while they discussed their next move.

"What's next, guys?" Bridget asked. "I think we ought to take a balloon ride tomorrow as a little escape from the heavy conversation. I bet we could enjoy some amazing scenery this side of 1828."

"You Americans are so laid back," Babette observed. "I think that is a splendid idea, Bridget. We could use a 'break,' as you say."

That night, Beauregard fixed a wonderful spaghetti and meatball dinner. Everybody feasted, then they all fell fast asleep, dreaming of the next day's events.

The next day was perfect for ballooning—the sky was clear and blue, there was brilliant sunshine and a steady breeze. Soon Bridget's jaws were working overtime, as she prepared to blow a giant bubble to carry them all off for a scenic tour.

As they soared high above the ground, the foursome saw the country change before their eyes. It was like watching a movie on fast forward. They see the United States grow larger, as Texas wins its independence from Mexico in 1836 and becomes a state in 1845. Then, in 1850 California becomes a state, likewise Oregon in 1859. But now they were seeing something even more dramatic: The states are dividing themselves between free states and slave states as they take sides over the slavery issue. It was a beautiful ride, but a troubling one, too. As Bridget began the slow descent to *Lady Liberty*, they realized that it was no longer 1828—it was 1860 and the country was on the verge of civil war.

"Wow! That was some trip! What happened up there?" Bridget said, when she could talk again. "I could see the country change right before my eyes but there was no time machine."

"I experienced the same phenomenon," Barnaby reported. "I have no idea how it happened but it was incredible. It was amazing to see all that growth and development, but very sad to see people preparing to fight one another."

"Is it true that brother fought brother in the Civil War?" Babette asked. "I could see families being split apart by the slavery issue."

"Yeah. It's hard to believe, but the war divided families, states, the whole country! Maybe it's time for a trip back home. We could regroup and check out the Civil War once we know what we want to see. What do you think? I'll bet ole Tempus Fugit will be happy to see us!"

"I'm not so sure about that," Barnaby answered. "After all, he thought we were spies trying to get the secrets of the time machine out of him! I wonder what he's doing now? But I guess we should be getting back, at least for a little while."

Back inside the ship, Barnaby set the tempometer for the present, and they all strapped themselves in for the trip. They were excited about the prospect of getting home, but they were eager to see more of the past, too.

Within moments, they were back in Dr. Tempus Fugit's laboratory and happily preparing to disembark when Bridget noticed something unusual.

"Where's Beauregard?" she asked nervously. "Has he already left the ship?"

But the main cabin hatch hadn't been touched. Bridget, Barnaby, and Babette looked at each other.

"Well, I guess we better reset for 1860 and go back and get him," Barnaby said.

"Not so fast!" said a voice from the hatchway. "I've been waiting to nab you the second you tried to come home, and now I've got you! All of you except that feline spy friend of yours! Where is he?" It was Dr. Tempus Fugit and he had a mixture of relief and anger written across his face.

"He got left behind," Bridget said sadly. "We've got to go back and get him! Now, before it's too late!"

"Forget that for the moment. You'll not be heading anywhere until I find out more about where you've been and where you want to go. After all, you're talking about traveling during wartime and that's hazardous duty! I'll forget about the spy thing, for now at least, if you'll tell me all about your adventures. I've been on pins and needles since you left!"

"Oooh, Dr. Tempus Fugit, I am so sorry that you have had pins and needles stuck into you while we were gone," Babette said comfortingly. "Can I get you medical assistance?"

"No, no! I mean I was very anxious for your safe return. You've been gone for an hour or so and I thought you'd be back right away," Dr. Tempus Fugit replied.

Barnaby, Babette, and Bridget looked at one another again. "An hour or so?" Barnaby said. "We do have to talk, Dr. Tempus! We have a lot to talk about, believe me!"

"Hold on just a minute!" Bridget cried. "I am *not* going to be happy until Beauregard is back with us. Let's devise a rescue operation while we bring Dr. Tempus up to date."

Back in 1860, Beauregard watched as the time machine shimmered like a bowl of Jell-o and vanished into thin air. He knew they'd be back, but then he had a few things to do before they returned to get him. "Now, where should I begin?" he thought.

✍ QUIZ #3 ✍
Exploring the New Frontier

1. The United States agreed to pay fifteen million dollars to France for what parcel of land?

2. What two explorers did President Jefferson send to explore the new territory purchased from France?

3. What was the name of the Native American woman who helped lead American explorers over the Rocky Mountains and on to the Pacific Ocean?

4. The United States and Great Britain went to war over the control of the high seas. What was this war called?

5. What Native American chief became an ally of the British in an attempt to drive American settlers away from Native American hunting grounds?

6. What was the name of the general who defeated the Native Americans and the British and became the seventh president of the United States?

7. After their defeat, Native Americans were forced to relocate to Oklahoma. What was their long, difficult journey called?

8. What president believed that the United States should stretch "from sea to shining sea?"

9. What is the belief that the United States was fated to expand from the Atlantic Ocean to the Pacific Ocean called?

10. Which state won its independence from Mexico in 1836?

✍ FOOD FOR THOUGHT ✍

Respond to any of the following questions that interest you in your journal. For some of the answers you will need to look in other sources, and some of the questions have many possible answers. Give them a try!

1. Why was France so willing to sell the Louisiana territory to the United States?

2. Was Great Britain's policy of the "impressment of sailors" justified? What did it have to do with the 1812 war?

3. In this chapter, there was some discussion about animals and their use by humans for food, clothing, shelter, etc. What do you think are the differences between our use of animals today and the way pioneers and Native Americans used animals? Are there limits to ways animals should be used? If humans have rights, do animals have rights, too?

4. Why did Andrew Jackson insist that Native Americans be moved to the western United States, even though it meant giving up their homes and farms? Do you think his policy was justified? How do Native Americans feel about his decision?

✍ **GROUP INVESTIGATIONS** ✍

These activities will help you find out more about exploring the frontier. You can do them with a small group, or by yourself if you prefer. Have fun!

1. Investigate Native American culture. Pick a tribe or tribes and investigate what foods they ate, what clothing they wore, what their lives were like. Create a Native American meal or a model of a village for the tribe you selected.

2. Who was Sequoya? Why is he important to Native American culture? Give examples of his accomplishments.

3. Gather some information about the Lewis and Clark expedition. What was life like on the pioneer trail? Draw a picture or write a story about their trip. Stage a skit, complete with costumes, or write a song or rap to add to the skit.

4. Investigate the Trail of Tears. Why did so many Native Americans die along the way? Write a poem, story, or song about their experiences.

Chapter 5
Beauregard's Return

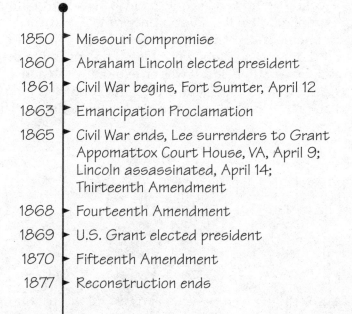

1850	Missouri Compromise
1860	Abraham Lincoln elected president
1861	Civil War begins, Fort Sumter, April 12
1863	Emancipation Proclamation
1865	Civil War ends, Lee surrenders to Grant Appomattox Court House, VA, April 9; Lincoln assassinated, April 14; Thirteenth Amendment
1868	Fourteenth Amendment
1869	U.S. Grant elected president
1870	Fifteenth Amendment
1877	Reconstruction ends

Well, as you can imagine, all that talk about furs and pelts was no picnic for me. What do people expect me to do, step out of my skin and hand it to them? The very idea!

Anyway, the Native Americans we met later certainly showed more respect for me, which made me feel a little better. Then, of course, my human friends forgot me and left me stranded in the past. Well, actually, that's not quite accurate. The truth is that I really chose to stay behind. You see, I had some business of a personal nature that required my attention...

"**I** can't believe your good fortune," Dr. Tempus Fugit was saying as they finished dinner. "You actually met Jefferson, Franklin, and Washington? Lewis and Clark? Andrew Jackson? Incredible!"

"That's right, Doc. We met some big names and we're going to meet some more!" Bridget was excited and worried at the same time. "But right now, I'd just like to figure out how to rescue Beauregard before we lose him altogether."

"I have a feeling your friend is quite able to take care of himself," Dr. Tempus replied. "He'll find you once you've returned to the 1860s. Just remember, the Civil War lasted four years and nearly six hundred thousand soldiers were killed, so you must be very careful to avoid the battlefields. It was an extremely sad and painful episode in American history, and it took the country a long time to recover from the destruction caused by the war. So, choose your path carefully!"

"I did not realize that so many people died in the Civil War," Babette said. "And why did it last so long?"

"I remember some of the big names like President Abraham Lincoln and the generals, Ulysses S. Grant and Robert E. Lee," Barnaby interjected. "I remember, too, that the North was much better prepared to fight the war because it had more people, more factories, and more railroads."

"Yeah, that's right," Bridget added. "I know that the slavery issue got so hot that there had to be compromises about admitting new states. There was one called the Missouri Compromise, which said states above a certain latitude were to be free states and states south of the latitude were to be slave. As you'd expect, it wasn't very effective."

"Maybe we should ask the computer for additional information," Barnaby suggested. "I mean, what really caused the war to break out in the first place?"

Dr. Tempus Fugit asked the computer for more information and the kids began to discuss their findings among themselves. They liked to put their heads together to figure out the best solution to a problem. It helped them to see alternatives and choose the best one available.

"The Missouri Compromise didn't solve the problem of admitting new states. Everybody was fighting over the latitude line and no one was ready to abolish slavery. Southerners generally favored slavery and Northerners generally wanted it abolished. There was a famous journalist, William Lloyd Garrison, who published a newspaper called *The Liberator.* The newspaper helped to mobilize support for the abolitionist movement in the North. People like Harriet Tubman, a former slave who escaped to the North, helped other slaves escape to Canada via the Underground Railroad. In the South, politicians argued that each state had the right to decide whether it was to be free or slave. So, from 1850 to 1860, everybody was taking sides on the issues of slavery and the states' rights. It was definitely a time when people on both sides were beyond compromise." Bridget decided to catch her breath for a minute before she continued.

"Wait a minute," said Barnaby. "I remember that there were differences in the soil and climate conditions in the North and South, too. Slavery was not as profitable in the North as it was in the South. The North had developed industry, especially with all the immigrant labor that came through New York City, while the South was still mostly rural and dependent on farming. So, slavery flourished in the South and gradually disappeared in the North."

"And is it not true that some of the Southern states threatened to leave the Union if Abraham Lincoln was elected president in

1860?" Babette asked. "I am not certain, but I think it was because Lincoln opposed slavery. Is that correct?"

"That's correct, Babette! The Southern states threatened to secede if Lincoln won the election," Bridget said. "And when he did, South Carolina voted to leave the Union. Ten more Southern states also left and organized the Confederate States of America, but in his inaugural speech Lincoln said that no state had the right to leave the Union. That was March 1861. On April 12, 1861, Confederate troops opened fire on Fort Sumter in the harbor of Charleston, South Carolina and the Civil War began."

"I still cannot understand why it lasted four years," Babette said. "If Barnaby is right, the North had all the advantages and the South had very few."

"I know what you're saying, Babette, and I really don't know the answer," Barnaby replied. "I guess we'll find out once we get to talk to a few key people. It's also puzzling that the country took such a long time to recover from the war."

"I don't know about you guys, but I'm ready to roll," Bridget interrupted. "Come on! Beauregard's waiting for us!"

A look of concern crossed Dr. Tempus Fugit's face. "I hope you know the difference between gray and blue! The Union soldiers, often called Yankees, wore blue uniforms. The Confederate soldiers, often called Rebels, wore gray uniforms. Bridget, be careful that your Yankees cap isn't misinterpreted by Confederate troops or all of you might be taken for spies. I seem to recall that I thought you were spies at first," he added, smiling at the memory. He really had grown quite fond of these young people and he was worried about their safety.

"Don't worry so much, Doc!" Bridget laughed. "We're usually in some kind of jam but we always manage to get out it. You'll see."

The three friends headed back to *Lady Liberty* and set the tempometer for 1861. Dr. Tempus waved farewell. "I'll be waiting to hear more stories when you return. And I'll bet Beauregard is waiting for you when you arrive!"

The time machine's warp drive worked without a glitch. When the lights had stopped shimmering in the main cabin, the kids peeked out of the viewer to find they were sitting in the middle of a cotton field. They popped the hatch and walked out into a hot summer's day in 1861. They couldn't see a soul for miles.

"It's so beautiful—I never realized how big these cotton fields were," Bridget said, scanning the field. "It must take weeks to pick all this cotton by hand."

They began to make their way toward the edge of the field, leaving *Lady Liberty* parked in the middle. They headed in the direction of the surrounding forest—this way they could avoid detection as well as escape the blazing sun. They soon reached the edge of the forest, where the cool cover of the forest canopy put them temporarily at ease. They sat down under a tree to relax and to decide on their next move.

"We must be near a farm or plantation somewhere in the South, having landed in a cotton field," Barnaby concluded. "Maybe we should find the owners and find out exactly where we are."

"Do you think anybody will ask questions about me?" Bridget asked thoughtfully. "I mean, I am African American and they might wonder why I am wandering around in the middle of a cotton field. I wouldn't want to attract unwanted attention to us."

"Your Yankees cap might do a better job of attracting unwanted attention than anything else," Barnaby replied. "Maybe you ought to stash it until we get north, just to be on the safe side."

"You can trash that idea," Bridget said emphatically. "This cap is me and I won't part company with it! End of discussion."

"Please, no arguments," Babette said calmly. "We need to figure a way out of this forest. We cannot see where we are going."

"Great idea, Frenchie!" Bridget said suddenly. "We'll balloon above the treetops for a better view, then decide the best way to go. How's that grab you?"

"It sounds like fun to me," Babette said, "even though I do not remember making that suggestion."

"I agree," Barnaby declared. "Let's move back to the edge of the field so we can catch a breeze. And we don't want to get caught up in the trees."

Bridget blew a beautiful pink bubble that slowly lifted them off the ground and they floated gracefully above the treetops, just as they had planned. It really was a beautiful day—blue, blue sky, not a cloud to be seen and very, very warm.

Suddenly, something quite important occurred to Barnaby. "You know, Bridget," he yelled, "I just realized that we don't have Beauregard's weight to add to the ballast. Since it's so warm, the air inside the balloon might expand and carry us too high. You might have to let some air out to keep us at a lower altitude."

Bridget carefully calculated how much air she needed to release in order to adjust the ballast. Meanwhile, they continued to soar higher and higher into the air. Then, without warning, a stiff breeze blew them to the east and they found themselves over water. From the shape of the shore line, Barnaby ventured a guess about their location.

"We're over the Atlantic Ocean, that's for sure, and I think that's South Carolina below us. Bridget, can you get us lower?" Barnaby crooked his neck so he could see his friend, whose face was now beginning to look a little red and strained.

"Look!" Babette interjected, as she pointed back toward the land. "We are passing over a city and there appears to be an island with some kind of fort in the harbor. I wonder if..."

She never got a chance to finish her sentence. As the kids watched with dismay, a formation of pelicans flew close to the bubble and suddenly a large beak poked a hole in its side. They heard the horrible sound that strikes fear into the heart of every balloonist in flight: Hisssssssssss.

It was a slow leak and Bridget was trying desperately to compensate, but she was losing the battle. They began a slow descent into the ocean. Babette and Barnaby looked at each other, looked down, and yelled to Bridget to blow harder.

"Hang in there, Bridget!" Barnaby called. "We might make land with just a little more air."

"We know you can do it," Babette shouted. "Show us some of that Yankee ingenuity!"

"And don't forget to hide that cap before you hit the ground! After all, this is Charleston, South Carolina and they'll think you're a Yankee spy from Fort Sumter."

Babette and Barnaby looked beneath them again. They were getting very close to the water but land was still within reach.

Bridget was trying to talk with her mouth full. "Wo sad wht?" she managed to mutter.

"What? What did you say?" Barnaby yelled. "I can't understand you."

"I think she's asking who made that last comment about the Yankee cap," Babette explained. "I thought you said it."

"Not me," Barnaby replied. "Wasn't it you?"

"No." Babette looked a little puzzled.

Then they both looked down and yelled, "Beauregard!" Just as they were skimming the waves, there was their fearless friend waiting to rescue them from the salty soup.

"When I count to three," he called up to them, "deflate the balloon and drop. Ready? One, two, three…Drop!"

Bridget popped her own bubble and they fell directly into the boat that Beauregard had waiting beneath them. It really was an amazing catch, but by now you'd have to say that Beauregard was used to saving these kids from peril.

Bridget felt like she had lockjaw but she was so happy to see Beauregard that she soon forgot all about it. Babette and Barnaby were still babbling about the rescue as Beauregard calmly rowed them toward shore.

When they reached the beach, they all embraced in a big circular hug. It was so good to be together again.

Bridget was full of questions. "How did you get here? How did you know we were coming? Where are you staying?" She was almost out of breath when Beauregard interrupted her.

"One question at a time, please!" he laughed. "I'll fill you in as quickly as possible. When you vanished, I decided here was my opportunity to investigate my past. After all, my heritage goes back generations in South Carolina and I couldn't resist the temptation to see my great, great, great, great grandfather, Beaufort, in the fur.

"Well, I found out that he was the favorite pet of a Confederate general named Pierre Gustave Toutant Beauregard who fought in every major battle of the Civil War, from Fort Sumter to Richmond. So, I made my way to Fort Sumter to find General Beauregard and Beaufort. As it turns out, we are here just before the Confederates fired on Fort Sumter. Well, I was scanning the skies with a pair of field glasses when I saw your pink bubble high in the air. I knew immediately that you were headed my way, so I secured a boat and rowed out to meet you. Oh, yes, Beaufort and I have become great friends. We have caroused a little with a few of his buddies, but I am afraid things are getting too hot to hang out together much longer."

"Your general friend sounds French, if I am not mistaken," Babette mused. "Where was he born?"

"He was born in Louisiana near New Orleans and was a West Point graduate before he resigned from the U.S. Army and joined the Confederate army after Louisiana seceded from the Union. It seems that quite a few Confederate generals resigned their commissions to fight for the Confederacy, including Robert E. Lee. We can talk more about that later. How about something to eat right now?"

Everybody enthusiastically agreed, and Beauregard escorted them back to the modest quarters he had rented. When they had finished eating, Babette and Barnaby had a few questions.

"You said the situation is difficult here, but I am not sure I understand what you mean," Babette said. "Has the war started yet?"

"Not yet," Beauregard replied, "but it won't be long. The Confederate troops are ready to fire on the Union troops stationed at Fort Sumter, the fort you saw while you were ballooning."

No sooner had Beauregard finished than the boom of cannon fire rattled the little floral dishes in the pantry. They all jumped to their feet and ran to the windows. Confederate troops had begun to shell Fort Sumter! It was April 12, 1861 and the Civil War was underway.

"What do we do now?" Bridget asked nervously. "Are we in the line of fire? Maybe we should get out of here!"

"You're absolutely right," Barnaby said. "We need to move out of Charleston and back to *Lady Liberty* as quickly as possible."

Beauregard was full of stories but it was not seeming like a good time to tell them. He felt very sad at having to leave Beaufort and his friends behind, almost like he was deserting them when they needed him most.

"It must have been a difficult decision for people who were loyal to their states," he reflected. "Robert E. Lee, the Confederacy's best general, was opposed to slavery but fought for the South because of his loyalty to Virginia."

"Is that why the war lasted so long?" Babette inquired once again. "Was it because the South had so many leaders who were committed to the Confederate cause? I keep asking that question but no one seems to know the answer."

"Well, that is one reason," Beauregard replied. "Another reason could be the lack of good military leadership on the Union side. President Lincoln wanted Lee to command his troops but Lee became commander of the Confederate army. Lincoln then tried several commanders before he found Ulysses S. Grant."

"Do you think Lee's decision to fight for the Confederacy actually prolonged the war?" Bridget asked. "I know Lee was considered an honorable and courageous man for making a tough decision. I guess I'm not sure he made the right choice, though, when you consider the consequences."

"That's a good point, Bridget," Barnaby replied. "I don't know if we have enough evidence to answer your question. Maybe we'll get a chance to ask him!"

"I do think it might be time to get out of this situation. The cannon fire is growing in intensity," Beauregard said nervously. "It's time to retreat!"

They headed out into the cobblestone streets of Charleston, the rumble of cannon fire in the background. But they were not entirely sure of the way back to *Lady Liberty*.

"Well, we ballooned in, so we could balloon out! My jaws are back in shape, and we could get out of here really quickly," Bridget suggested.

"I think we'd better take a land route with all this cannon fire around. We'd be great target practice for either side," Barnaby replied.

"I think I know a way out of the city," Beauregard said, "but you might have to scoot down some narrow alleyways and over a few fences. Beaufort showed me some very interesting ways to get around town."

"I would rather take the alleys than the airways," Babette giggled. "We would certainly see more of the city."

"Follow me, then," Beauregard whispered, and off they went, single file, through the back streets and alleys of Charleston. After they had been moving along at a fast pace for a while, Bridget called for a breather.

"Hey, let's take a rest in that park over there," she panted. "This place is too beautiful to believe."

The foursome lay down in the young grass to enjoy the splendid day, even though they knew a war had started. The warm breeze and blue sky helped them to forget their troubles, at least for now. Beauregard took advantage of the moment by curling up for a quick nap. When he awoke ten minutes later, the group was ready to strike out for the cotton fields.

As they picked themselves up from the grass, however, the bushes suddenly came alive with Confederate soldiers! They surrounded the time travelers and began to ask questions.

"Excuse me, ma'am, but we'd like to know where you got that hat you're wearin'." The commanding officer looked warily at Bridget. "We've been hearin' rumors of Yankee infiltrators in the area and we aim to round 'em up and hold them for questioning."

"Hold your horses there, Sir," Bridget cried. "My cap might say 'Yankees' on it, but it's not the same Yankees you're thinking about. Why, this cap is a genuine souvenir of *the* greatest baseball team on the face of the earth! So why don't you guys just go find some real Yankees to pick on!"

"Sorry, ma'am, but y'all are dressed kinda funny and your story sounds just a little fishy to us. Now would you mind tellin' us where you're from? And who are your people?" The officer obviously wanted some answers he could understand.

"Well, I'm from New York City and that's where the Yankees play ball," Bridget said seriously. "C'mon, you guys don't know who the Yankees are? You must be living in a time warp or something."

"Well, little lady, you just said a mouthful there!" the soldier laughed. "If you say you're from New York, you've got to be a Yankee! I reckon we'll have to bring you in for questioning. Come along peaceably now, please. We don't want any trouble. If you're innocent, we'll let you go. But you better come up with a better explanation for that hat!"

"Nice going, Bridget!" Barnaby whispered. "We told you that hat was going to be trouble. Now we're headed to the stockade, and we may never get out!"

"Chill, Barnaby," Bridget said calmly. "This cap is a good luck charm, and I *know* we'll be all right as long as I'm wearing it."

"Oooh, good luck charms! You Americans are so funny about hats. Don't you pull rabbits out of hats, too?" Babette said. What a time to be joking!

"Magicians do a trick where they pull a rabbit out of a hat, Babette, and it might take a magician to get us out of this fix," Barnaby worried.

Beauregard remained cool, calm, and collected as they walked down the street toward the Confederate compound. He already had a plan. If he could only get a message to Beaufort. He just needed a distraction of some sort in order to escape his captors.

"Magic, superstition, hmmmm," he thought to himself. "I wonder if the old black cat routine would work on these soldiers."

Suddenly, Beauregard, who had not spoken a word since his nap in the grass, let out a mighty loud RROWWRLLLL, arched his back, and spiked his fur. The whole entourage came to an abrupt halt.

"'Scuse me, ma'am, but your cat friend seems agitated about something. Any idea what's upsettin' him?" one of the soldiers asked Bridget.

"Well, I guess it's because you crossed his path," Bridget said matter-of-factly. "You know it's bad luck for a black cat to cross your path, don't you?"

The soldiers looked at one an other. "We really don't need any bad luck right now so maybe we ought to just let him be, don't you think, Captain?" one of the soldiers said.

The Confederate officer eyed the situation carefully and judged his men to be more alarmed than Beauregard. He spoke reassuringly. "Now men, you're not goin' to let an old superstition get you riled up, are you? I mean, this is just a cat—a pretty big one with a nice shiny coat, I'll admit—but a cat nonetheless. So, how is it he's supposed to bring us bad luck?"

Beauregard suddenly stood on his hind legs, bowed graciously, and spoke to the officer. "Why Captain, I trust you recognize good South Carolina stock when you see it. You might even know a relative of mine by the name of Beaufort? My name is Beauregard and I was named after the Confederate general who I believe you know quite well. I believe it would be very bad luck if he finds out that you've arrested me."

"Beggin' your pardon, Sir. I am Captain Buck Stonewall and these men are new recruits. We got a little upset about your friend's hat, but I know that someone of your breeding would not be involved with spies. Could we perhaps be of some assistance?"

"As a matter of fact, my friends and I were just leaving when the hostilities broke out. Perhaps you could give us proper directions?" Beauregard inquired.

Captain Stonewall gave the group exit directions and bade them farewell, apologizing for the delay once again. As the foursome resumed their journey, they breathed a sigh of relief. They were back on track!

"We can't be far away now!" Bridget said excitedly. "Look over there! I think that's the trail that leads to the cotton field."

Bridget, Babette, Barnaby, and Beauregard were happy to spot *Lady Liberty* still sitting amidst the cotton. She was looking a bit dusty, but apart from a bird or two no one else seemed to have found her.

Once on board, they discussed their next move. First they went to the computer and asked for more data on the Civil War. Then it was time to make a decision.

"We have lots of options," Barnaby began. "Maybe we could

visit some of the major battlefields like Gettysburg, Vicksburg, or Richmond."

"I want to meet Lee and Grant," Bridget declared. "I really want to see the country get through the war and begin to rebuild."

"I agree with Bridget," Babette said. "We could go to the peace talks and watch a new beginning. I would learn more about the war that way, I think. Besides, I would prefer to avoid any violence."

"I see your point," Barnaby reflected. "We could move on to more productive moments rather than dwell on the battles. So, let's see, we need to be at Appomattox Court House, Virginia, on April 9, 1865."

"Yeah, let's get out of here," Bridget agreed, yanking her cap farther down on her head.

Barnaby set the tempometer for the exact date and flicked the switch.

When they looked out the viewer a few moments later, they saw the armies of gray and blue in opposing camps and the small courthouse cabin where Lee and Grant were discussing the terms of the surrender. It was a poignant conclusion to a terrible event in American history. The mood of the scene was peaceful, the peace that comes with exhaustion.

Before the time travelers went to met Lee and Grant, they decided to find out more about the terms of Lee's surrender. They hooked into the computer again and discovered that Ulysses S. Grant had earned the nickname "Unconditional Surrender Grant" after he had taken charge of the Union Army in 1864. Lee, on the other hand, was looking for terms that would allow his men to return to their homes and start anew. Grant had hammered away at the South, and his colleague, General Sherman, had burned a forty-mile-wide swath from Atlanta, Georgia, to the Atlantic Ocean, which effectively demoralized the Confederates. Grant caught up with Lee after the fall of Richmond, the Confederate capital, at Appomattox. His men surrounded the Confederate Army, finally bringing an end to the conflict.

President Abraham Lincoln had been busy, too. He had fought the war to preserve the Union, but he could not find the military leadership he needed to defeat the Confederates and restore the

Union. He had issued the Emancipation Proclamation on January 1, 1863, freeing the slaves in the rebellious states and allowing African Americans to enlist in the Union Army and Navy. He had also penned one of the most elegant speeches in the history of America, the Gettysburg Address, as a dedication to the forty thousand men who were killed on the battlefield at Gettysburg in the crucial turning point of the war. President Lincoln's call for the benevolent reconstruction of the South emphasized his belief that the Union must be restored without punishing the South for its rebellion. He was assassinated five days after Lee's surrender on April 14, 1865 by John Wilkes Booth. Reconstruction would be far from benevolent. Andrew Johnson succeeded Lincoln and attempted to follow his predecessor's approach to reconstruction but was almost impeached for taking this position.

Bridget, Babette, Barnaby, and Beauregard approached the courthouse window and peered in at the two exhausted generals. Then they went around to the door, tapped lightly, and went inside.

"I wonder if we might have a word with you gentlemen as you deliberate about the future of the Union and the Confederacy," Beauregard began.

There was a long silence. Lee and Grant did not seem receptive to the idea. They invited Beauregard to sit with them at the table,

however, as a gesture of goodwill, but Bridget, Barnaby, and Babette had to be content with observing from a spot near the window.

The mood at the table was businesslike but conciliatory. Lee was assured that his men could keep their horses but the Confederate Army had to be disbanded and the men had to relinquish their weapons. Lee was a gentleman, a man of honor who kept his word, and Grant knew that he would live up to his commitments. Beauregard listened intently as the men discussed the terms of the surrender but said nothing, feeling honored to witness such a historical moment. When he returned to his friends, they were strangely quiet.

"I am impressed with the dignity of the moment," Babette said. "I remember the Yorktown surrender, and this is somehow very sad. I am glad it is behind us."

"It isn't really behind us yet," Barnaby commented. "From what I've read, Lincoln's assassination turns reconstruction into a punishment rather than a reconciliation."

"I remember stuff about that," Bridget said, with sudden animation. "I've got my computer information right here. It should give us some understanding of what happened after the war. Let's see…Reconstruction fell into the hands of a group of legislators in Congress whom everybody called the 'Radical Republicans.' They divided the South into five military districts and each of the Southern states was readmitted to the Union as they accepted the Fourteenth Amendment (outlawing slavery) or the Fifteenth Amendment (civil rights for freed slaves) to the Constitution.

"Grant was elected president in 1869, and the end of his second term in office in 1877 marked the end of the Reconstruction period. Grant's presidency was troubled with scandals and charges of corruption, but then, the whole country seemed plagued with dishonesty. New state governments in the South resented the Freedmen's Bureau, an agency created by Congress to protect freed African Americans from abuse. Secret organizations like the Ku Klux Klan formed to terrorize people who supported the rights of freed slaves. But the worst problem still remained, once Reconstruction was over. Even though they were free, African American citizens in the South still did not own any land and that meant they had little money to support their new political rights. In time, Southern states passed laws and taxes to restrict the rights of African Americans. These restrictions were challenged by the civil rights movement in the fifties and sixties of the next century. So, it seems like Reconstruction was a big bust for the South, huh?"

"It would seem that way," Babette said. "But then, the aftermath of war is always terrible. But things did get better, yes?"

"Yes, they did," Beauregard said. "And you'll get to see some of the people who made modern life a reality just as soon as we jump to a new era. Are we ready?"

"Yeah!" the kids all answered together. They prepared themselves for another trip in *Lady Liberty*, more aware than ever before that the preservation of freedom sometimes requires a terrible price.

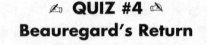

✍ QUIZ #4 ✑
Beauregard's Return

1. The Civil War started with the Confederate attack on what fortification?

2. What year did the Civil War begin and when did it end? How many lives were lost?

3. Who was the famous abolitionist whose newspaper helped to mobilize support against slavery?

4. What law admitted states to the Union according to whether they were north or south of a certain latitude?

5. The turning point of the Civil War was the Union's military victory at what place?

6. Who commanded the Confederate forces during the Civil War?

7. Which commander of the Union Army eventually became president for two terms during the Reconstruction period?

8. During Reconstruction, what agency was created to protect the rights of freed African Americans?

9. What was the name of the secret organization that terrorized and tortured freed African Americans and their supporters?

10. Which president was assassinated on 14 April 1865? Who killed him?

11. What former slave helped slaves escape from the South by the Underground Railroad?

✍ FOOD FOR THOUGHT ✍

Use your journal to write down your responses to any or all of the questions about the Civil War and Reconstruction. There are many possible answers. See if you can give reasons to support your answer!

If you need assistance, ask your librarian or teacher to help you find more information on the subject. Enjoy!

1. Do you think the Civil War was inevitable? Why or why not?

2. What was the argument for states' rights? How did it influence the Southern states' positions about slavery and about tariffs?

3. Was the Radical Republican approach to Reconstruction justified? Why or why not?

4. Why did Lincoln issue the Emancipation Proclamation? How did it influence the outcome of the Civil War?

5. Robert E. Lee chose to fight for the South in the Civil War. Some people think he helped to prolong the war when he made that decision. What do you think?

6. The failure of Reconstruction to provide land for freed African Americans made it difficult for them to exercise their political rights. Why? What is the connection between political rights and economics?

✍ GROUP INVESTIGATIONS ✍

You might enjoy doing some of these activities with your friends or family. Follow your interests and choose something fun!

1. Create Confederate Army and Union Army uniforms. Use the uniforms to stage a skit about an important battle or about the terms of the surrender at Appomattox Court House.

2. Draw a picture, write a story, song, or rap about the Civil War.

3. Would you have fought for the North or the South in the Civil War? Why?

4. What role did books like *Uncle Tom's Cabin* by Harriet Beecher Stowe play in the Civil War?

5. Do you think movies like *Gone With the Wind* give an accurate picture of what life was like for Southern women and for women of color?

6. What did Native Americans think of the Civil War? Did they play a role in the West?

Chapter 6
Machines!

1869 — First transcontinental railroad completed

1876 — Alexander Graham Bell invents the telephone

1877 — Reconstruction ends

1878 — Thomas Alva Edison invents the phonograph

1879 — Thomas Alva Edison invents the electric light bulb

1882 — Jan Metzeliger invents a shoe-making machine

1896 — Henry Ford utilizes the assembly line in automobile manufacturing; *Plessy v. Ferguson* decision by Supreme Court

1898 — Marie Curie discovers radium

1903 — The Wright Brothers fly at Kitty Hawk, N.C.

1914 — World War I begins in Europe

1918 — World War I ends

1920 — Nineteenth Amendment gives women the right to vote

1923 — Garrett Morgan invents the traffic light

I really think I distinguished myself at that last stop, don't you? In 1861, I performed a daring rescue at sea, met my ancestor in the fur, and found out more about my heritage. I always knew about Beaufort, but I never realized how Beauregard got to be a family name. I wish Bridget, Babette, and Barnaby had met Beaufort. He was really very much like the rest of my family—you know, black cats of historic proportions whose gentility is rather more than noteworthy. Anyway, I'm glad to be reunited with my human friends, ready for some more action! I think we're through dodging cannon fire for a while, thank goodness, so now we can visit some of America's great inventors. By the way, did I ever tell you about my own invention, the electric mousetrap? You might call it a way of producing instant crispy critters. Yum! But then, I digress...

✎ ✎ ✎ ✎ ✎

CLICK! HUMMM! "We're off!" shouted Barnaby, as the time machine leapt out of the cotton field and into a new era of ingenuity. "We're going to skip across the next forty years like a flat rock skimming across a still pond," Barnaby announced dramatically. "We've got some big names and amazing machines to check out."

"Who?" Bridget demanded. "We're not going to sit through years of boring lectures from old guys who look like they need a life, are we?"

Babette chuckled and said, "Why not? I think it would be charming to meet an interesting and highly intelligent inventor. You are not excited?"

Bridget frowned. "It's just that they can be a little crazy. I mean, look at Dr. Tempus Fugit. How would you like to listen to an explanation of the math he used to invent *Lady Liberty*? Not!"

Barnaby winced. "Pleassse! I listen to your boring baseball banter, which is far more banal than a math lecture! Mathematics is the language of the sciences."

"Wait a minute! Baseball batting averages are statistics and statistics are mathematical computations. So there!" Bridget was not about to let Barnaby feel like he was some sort of genius, even though he acted pretty weird himself sometimes.

"Which inventors are we going to visit?" Babette asked, changing the subject. "There are so many possibilities!"

"Well, I thought we'd like to meet the guy who created our favorite invention," Barnaby replied. "You know, the one people say grows attached to our ears because we're on it all the time!"

Bridget and Babette laughed and said, "The telephone!"

"That is correct, my friends," Barnaby chuckled.

So, they set the time machine for 1876, the year Alexander Graham Bell first exhibited his amazing invention. After a short hop, the foursome arrived, ready to meet the man who had made it possible for them to talk to one another for hours, even though they had been together only minutes earlier.

"Where are we?" Bridget asked. "It looks like we've headed north this time."

"We're in Boston, I think," Barnaby said. "Look over there! That must be Bell's laboratory, judging from all the hoopla going on."

"Well, let's join the party," Bridget said and scampered across the street from the park where they had landed. *Lady Liberty* looked like a newly erected statue in the middle of the freshly clipped lawn. But no one even noticed her. The crowds were milling all around the exhibition hall and lines had formed to catch a glimpse of the new invention.

"Should we squeeze inside to see if we can talk with Alexander Graham Bell?" Babette said to her friends.

"Where's Beauregard?" Bridget asked suddenly. "Has he slipped off again? I can never seem to keep track of him."

"Let's go inside," Barnaby suggested. "Maybe he's waiting for us there."

They worked their way inside and stopped to read a poster announcing that a public demonstration of Mr. Bell's invention would take place in the auditorium in a short while.

"Hmmm, we might as well attend the demonstration. I don't see Beauregard anywhere, do you?" Barnaby asked.

"I bet he's up to something," Bridget replied. "Come on, let's go check out Mr. Bell. I guess Beauregard will catch up with us later."

"Will he know where to find us?" Babette worried. "This is a big place."

"He probably knows more about where we are than we do," Bridget laughed. "Looks like the demonstration has already started. Let's take a seat."

Alexander Graham Bell was speaking from the stage as they entered. He held a contraption in his hands that didn't resemble a telephone at all.

Babette whispered to Barnaby, "I do not recognize that device he is holding. And his accent, it is very distinct."

Barnaby smiled. "It's a Scottish accent. I guess he must be an immigrant. And that thing that looks like a torture device is actually the inside of the very first telephone. Amazing."

Bridget had been listening while the other two whispered. "Listen up, over there!" she said, nudging Barnaby in the ribs. "This guy used to run a school here in Boston for training teachers of the deaf. His father and grandfather were both pioneers in speech therapy. It seems he got interested in the ways deaf people can learn to speak and began to experiment with using electricity to transmit sound. He said he worked on this invention for years."

While Bridget was explaining what the other two had missed, Alexander Graham Bell had gotten a volunteer from the audience. When the three kids looked up, they yelled in unison, "Beauregard!" The crowd turned to look at them and murmured disapprovingly following their outburst.

Suddenly, a member of the audience shouted at Mr. Bell, "What're you doin' with a cat on the stage? Cats can't talk! They're barely able to recognize their own names when you call them! Get a human being, for Pete's sake!"

"Who is Pete?" Babette wondered. But she never got a chance to ask her comrades. There was a sudden shriek of shock from the audience as Beauregard stood on his hind legs, and began to talk.

"Excuse me, Mr. Rude, but I am a highly educated cat from a well-respected family. You might refrain from passing judgment so quickly in the future!"

Pandemonium broke loose as soon as Beauregard finished speaking. His speech had given the local folks a terrible shock, and within seconds they were stampeding toward the exits! Alexander Graham Bell and his volunteer stood mystified on the stage.

Mr. Bell did not look happy. "I thought you would be the perfect subject," he began. "You would respond to a human voice over the telephone as if you had been beckoned by your owner. Instead, you suddenly start to speak! My stars! Where did you come from? A talking cat!"

"Maybe I should be moving along," Beauregard said apologetically. "My friends and I merely wanted to meet you but I'm afraid we've caused you some difficulty. Please forgive the intrusion."

"That's it!" Mr. Bell said suddenly. "You and your friends must have some kind of ventriloquist act that you're trying to showcase. I can't believe you used *my* audience to attract attention to yourselves! Why, you are all dressed very much like show people. I've guessed it, haven't I?"

Suddenly, Beauregard dropped to all fours and began to meow like a typical house cat. Bridget took the cue immediately.

"That's right, Mr. Bell!" she said with a smile. "You're pretty clever to have figured that out. We do apologize for the inconvenience, but we'll be on our way now." They began to move toward the nearest exit.

"Wait! It's true you've been a terrible nuisance, but I'm fascinated by your incredible talent. How did you get your cat to talk so realistically? And he walks remarkably well on his hind legs. Can you explain these phenomena to me?"

"Well, I tell you what, Mr. Bell, we'll have to discuss it some other time. Those people appear to be regrouping outside, and I don't think they're feeling quite so friendly now. We'd better get out of here before there's trouble."

Bell picked up on the sense of urgency in Bridget's voice. "Quickly, out the back door," he urged. "When you get out of the building, turn right and follow the alley. It'll bring you out by the park. I'll try to hold off the mob with my telephone demonstration. Good luck!"

As they ran past Alexander Graham Bell, the time travelers bade him farewell and thanked him for his help. "Keep up the good work!" Bridget yelled as they headed down the alley. "I'm sure you'll be a great success!"

They arrived at the edge of the park and dashed toward *Lady Liberty*, reaching her threshold without a problem. Once inside, they collapsed in a heap on the floor.

"I think we should get out of here before someone starts asking more questions," Barnaby said. "How about the phonograph or the light bulb? We could visit Thomas Alva Edison's laboratory. He's only a couple of years down the road."

"How do you know about all these inventors?" Bridget asked.

"I have always been interested in inventions," Barnaby replied. "You remember my apartment in Paris? It was my laboratory. I'd lock myself in there for days experimenting with new ideas. And I read up on some of the big names because I wanted to know more about their contributions to science."

"I remember your laboratory very well," Babette said. "But then you blew it up with your famous fermenting sock experiment. I hope we will not encounter another experiment like that!"

"No worries," Barnaby laughed. "Thomas Edison's laboratory was like wonder world. He produced so many different inventions that it's difficult to keep track of them all. He even helped to improve Bell's original telephone so that it could be used in a more practical fashion."

"Fascinating," Babette replied. "Where do we meet this science wizard?"

"Let's try 1879 at Menlo Park, New Jersey. That's the time and place he invented the first light bulb. We might even catch him at work on some other ideas."

"This guy sounds interesting," Bridget said enthusiastically. "Let's go!"

With a flick of the switch, *Lady Liberty* disappeared from 1876 and reappeared in 1879. The time travelers popped the hatch and stepped out into warm New Jersey sunshine.

"How are we going to find Thomas Edison?" Babette wondered aloud. "His laboratory could be miles from here! Why don't we ask that man if he knows the way?" Babette was pointing to a man standing on the edge of some farmland not far from their landing site. He was giving them a strange look.

As they walked up to ask for directions, the man began to mumble to himself. "Must be Edison playin' around with electricity again. Never seen anything like it!"

"Excuse me," Babette began. "We were wondering if you could direct us to Thomas Edison's laboratory. Is it close by?"

"I knew it! I just knew you had something to do with Edison. I've never seen anybody just appear like that before, you know. Thought I was seeing things! Tell me, are you French?"

Babette looked startled. "Yes, how did you know? Is it my accent?" she asked.

"No, it's that Statue of Liberty. The French are building a statue like that to give to the United States as a gift for our centennial celebration. But how did you get a smaller version before the original is even completed?"

"Ah, well, you know the French are very creative, and one of the things we enjoy creating the most is an air of mystery. I am afraid I cannot tell you any more than that," Babette responded dramatically and shut her mouth tight.

"Hmmm. Well, it is kind of hard to see you behind those dark glasses," the man replied. "And I wonder what Mr. Edison has to do with all this mystery stuff. I know, why don't I take you to his place? He lives right up the road here." The man pointed the way.

"Well, er...I guess that would be all right," Bridget interjected, "but we really don't know you. Why don't you just give us directions and we'll manage on our own."

"That's fine by me," replied the man. "If you follow this road for half a mile, you'll walk right into Edison's place! And tell him I sent you."

"Sure thing. Well, we'll be heading on up the road now," Bridget said warily. She looked at her friends and said under her breath, "C'mon, let's get going before Farmer Brown decides to get friendly again."

They enjoyed the walk through the fertile farmland and, just as Farmer Brown had said, walked right into Edison's place. They knocked on the door.

Bridget jumped back in shock. "It's Farmer Brown!" she shouted.

Thomas Edison laughed and said, "I'm sorry for startling you like that, but I'm careful about strangers in the vicinity of the lab...spies, you know."

"Actually, I believe this is the first time we haven't been mistaken for spies," Barnaby said. "Mr. Edison, we would really love to tour your laboratory, if you can spare a few moments for some interested travelers."

"Why yes! Please come in. I'll show you some of my latest efforts, provided you really aren't going to discuss them with other inventors. Come this way."

Thomas Edison's laboratory was a large area very similar to Dr. Tempus Fugit's, except there were no computers. He was obviously involved with the many uses of electricity—the workbenches were covered with all different kinds of wire and tubing. The kids and the cat were immediately enthralled by the spirit of creativity that filled the room.

Bridget was inspecting everything in sight. She spied an unusual-looking device that looked like a cylinder covered with tin foil that turned with a hand crank.

"What's this machine, Mr. Edison?" she inquired respectfully. "It almost looks like the insides of a music box."

"I'm still working on that one. I call it a phonograph or speaking machine," Edison replied. "If I crank the handle fast enough..."

Edison began to crank the handle and a scratchy voice became audible. It was Edison.

"Wow! What do you plan to do to improve it?" Barnaby asked. "It looks like a really interesting machine." Of course, Barnaby already knew the answer, but he didn't want Edison to become suspicious.

"I hope to use electricity to turn the crank. Then people could record all kinds of things, even music. It cost only eighteen dollars to make. I wish I could say that about my current invention. I spent over forty thousand dollars creating it."

Edison took the travelers over to his current invention. "What do you think?" he asked.

"What is it?" Babette inquired. "It looks like a light bulb of some sort."

"That's precisely what it is!" Edison exclaimed. "But I've got to improve the number of hours it burns," he said, rubbing his chin thoughtfully. "I'll keep trying different materials until I perfect it. Just think, with this invention homes and streets will no longer be dark at night. And I have many more plans for harnessing electricity."

"The light bulb is fascinating," Barnaby said, as he inspected the invention carefully. "But how will people use it if electricity isn't available? Houses don't have electricity now, do they?"

"Now young man, don't be silly! You know your home doesn't have electricity. But that's my next project—figuring out a system of wiring that will allow homes and businesses to receive electricity. Then, all kinds of inventions can be created to utilize it!"

It was then that the peculiar look came across Edison's face. "Say, you folks never did say where you came from. Judging from your clothing, you're not from around these parts. Now, I know this young lady is from France, but what about the rest of you?"

"Well, I'm from New York City," Bridget announced proudly. "And Beauregard and Barnaby are world citizens," she said, hoping to divert Edison's attention from the topic.

"World citizens. I like the sound of it, but what does it mean?" Edison responded. "Does it mean that you travel a great deal?"

"Precisely, Mr. Edison," Barnaby replied. "Can you show us one more promising invention before we go?"

Thomas Edison laughed. "Ah, the insatiable curiosity of the

young! Come, here's an idea I have yet to create. I hope to find a way of making pictures move once they have been linked on a roll of film. I think I'll call it a kinetoscopic camera. You'll be able to peep into a box and watch a film. What do you think of that idea?"

"Cool!" Bridget exploded. "So you're the guy who invented the motion picture?"

Bridget immediately realized her mistake. "I mean...you know, you're the guy who invented this camera thing you're talking about?"

Too late. Edison's eyes widened. "How did you know about my idea before I told you about it? Who are you? Are you from the government?"

"Mr. Edison, we are merely curious young travelers, nothing more," Babette responded calmly. "But perhaps we have taken too much of your valuable time." Then, looking at her companions, she said, "We should be leaving now."

Edison looked pretty skeptical, but he wanted to get back to work. "They might look a bit weird," he thought to himself, "but they don't really seem devious."

So, the foursome said good-bye and thank you, and started off toward the door. Edison stopped them when they reached the doorway. "Just a word of advice before you go," he said. "Follow your curiosity, your interests, and work hard to accomplish your goals. Even though I had only three months of schooling, I'm always learning. When you get back to your future, remember me as a person who never gave up."

With a smile and a wink, Edison shut the door, leaving the time travelers to ponder his parting words.

"Do you think he *knew*?" Bridget said in an audible whisper. "I mean, do you think he knew we are from the future?"

Barnaby shrugged. "We'll never know for sure, but I'm guessing that he knew from the very beginning. It's not surprising, though. Edison worked constantly for fifty years to create all kinds of inventions. He had over a thousand patents in his name. He's a remarkable man."

As Bridget, Babette, Barnaby, and Beauregard walked down the road toward *Lady Liberty*, they decided to plan their next stop. Their visits with Bell and Edison had been incredible, but now what?

"There is one person that I have always wanted to meet," Babette said thoughtfully. "He made automobiles cheap enough for his workers to buy them. Can you think of his name?"

"You must mean Henry Ford," Barnaby replied. "He was one of the industrial giants of his time. Yes, it would probably be very interesting to meet him."

"He might be a hard guy to find, though," Bridget said. "Wasn't he a real mechanical type, always tinkering around with engines and stuff?"

"I suppose he was," Babette said. "He made a car called the Model T and everybody in America bought one."

"Shall we see if we can find him?" Barnaby asked. "It will be our first visit to the twentieth century."

After the jolt of the time jump, Barnaby checked out the landscape. He returned to his comrades and reported a successful jump. "Well, it's 1908 and we're in Detroit, Michigan, and we couldn't have landed much closer to Henry Ford's factory. However, our arrival has created quite a stir. We've landed on the roof of a bank right across the street from Henry Ford's first assembly line. It looks like he's got some Model Ts for sale right outside the factory. Unfortunately, there's a crowd forming and they all think we're trying to rob the bank. So what do we do?"

"That's easy," Bridget replied. "We just ask to speak to Mr. Ford and introduce ourselves as prospective customers looking for a good trade-in. What do you think?"

"Trade in *Lady Liberty*?" Barnaby said incredulously. "How will we get home?"

"Oh, Barnaby, I don't *really* mean we're going to trade in the time machine," Bridget chuckled. "We're going to meet Henry Ford and get out of this jam we're in, that's all. Quick thinking, huh?"

"Oooh, you are so clever, Bridget," Babette cooed. "There is only one problem: What if they don't take trade-ins?"

"That's just a chance we'll have to take," Bridget said resolutely. "Let's get out of this machine and into the daylight."

Crawling out on top of the bank building, Bridget spotted the lean form of the person they wanted to meet joining the crowd.

"That's him, right there," she said, pointing into the crowd. Then, feeling bold, she called out, "Hey, Mr. Ford, you're the man we want to see. Can we talk?"

Mr. Ford sauntered out in front of the crowd and called back, "Sure, what do you want?"

"We'd like to see your automobile and see how it's made. We hear it's the latest innovation in cheap transportation. Is that true?"

"Well, I like to think so. My conveyor belt allows the automobiles to be assembled quickly and cheaply. I've priced them so that my workers can afford to buy them, if they want. I call it 'the Ford idea.' Still interested?"

"You bet," Bridget called back. "We're coming down."

With unusual grace, Bridget blew a beautiful pink bubble balloon and the foursome landed as delicately as butterflies in the street below, much to the amazement of the crowd.

"Okay, folks. The show's over," a policeman said from the sidelines. "This looks like another of Mr. Ford's advertising gimmicks to me."

The crowd slowly dispersed, leaving the time travelers alone with Henry Ford.

"How did you do that?" he asked Bridget. "You people would make a great advertisement for my automobile. Would you be interested in...?"

"Oh, no, Mr. Ford," Babette interrupted. "We are interested in you and your invention. Would you show us how you make an automobile?"

"Absolutely, young lady. I'll bet you'll be buying one of these beauties one day," Mr. Ford replied. "Come with me. You know, this automobile I call the Model T Ford is going to put America on wheels. As you enter the factory, please don't distract the workers from their tasks. It's very important for them to concentrate. Each person has a job to do, and I insist that he does it well. I pay top dollar—five dollars a day—and I demand my workers be thrifty and sober at all times."

The kids and the cat got to see the assembly line from start to finish. First, the chassis and wheels, then the engine, then the body and the interior were assembled right before their eyes. What made it even more interesting was that they knew this was all happening on the first conveyor belt ever created. The entire process took about two hours.

Mr. Ford watched the assembly line very closely. At times, he would interrupt a worker and show him how to perform his task more carefully.

Barnaby ventured a question. "Mr. Ford, how did you learn so much about making automobiles?

"Well, young man, that's a good question. You see, I built one myself in my barn. Everybody kept telling me that the automobile would never replace the horse because no one could afford to buy one. So, I decided to build one cheap enough for the average person to buy. Remember this: Time is money. If I can make cars more efficiently, I can sell them more cheaply. So, the assembly line is my way of producing automobiles more efficiently, enabling me to sell them more cheaply. Pretty radical economics for these times, eh?"

Bridget nudged Babette in the ribs and whispered, "This guy sure loves to hear himself talk, doesn't he?"

Babette noticed Mr. Ford give Bridget a quizzical look, and she decided to pretend Bridget had made a joke. She smiled politely at her friend and said, "Oh Bridget, you are so funny sometimes. But you should leave your jokes until later."

Bridget caught on pretty quickly, but not as fast as Henry Ford. "Jokes? You like jokes? I've got lots of them. Here, have a cigar," he said as he stuck one in Beauregard's mouth.

Before the startled cat could protest, Henry lit the cigar. Suddenly, there was a loud BAM! and Beauregard's beautiful whiskers and shiny black fur were covered with soot. The cigar had exploded—and Beauregard was not a happy cat. Henry Ford, however, laughed loudly at Beauregard's appearance. He loved practical jokes.

But Beauregard, being a cat of the world, had a little surprise of his own. "Very clever, Mr. Ford, but allow me to shake hands to show that there are no hard feelings," he said, extending his paw.

"Now that's a good sport!" Ford responded as he grabbed Beauregard's paw.

There was a loud buzzing sound and Henry Ford's face registered quite a shock. "YEOW!" he yelled, jerking his hand away and rubbing it furiously.

Beauregard smiled appreciatively and said, "Some practical jokes are not always in good taste, don't you think, Mr. Ford?"

"I see your point," Henry Ford replied. "Thanks for the hint. And now, if you'll excuse me, I must get back to work. I hope you all remember this visit and return to buy a Model T." He turned, waved, and walked back into the assembly line, looking at his watch again as he went.

"Wow!" Bridget said. "That guy is quite a dynamo. So much energy! It seems like all of these inventor types are unique individuals, know what I mean?"

"Yes, yes, I do," Barnaby replied. "It's an inspiration to meet these people. When we get back, I'm going straight to my new laboratory."

"Just as long as no dirty socks are involved, I think you'd be a great inventor," Bridget chuckled. "Hey, are we going to see the Wright brothers fly?"

"Well, that could be tricky," Barnaby said. "We'd have to go backward. We have to get to 1903 and the Outer Banks of North Carolina. It could be interesting because until now we've only traveled in one direction. Do you want to try going backward?"

"What happens if something goes wrong?" Babette asked cautiously. "Could we be trapped forever?"

"Who knows?" Bridget shrugged. "It could be instant primordial soup or we could see Orville and Wilbur fly. I'm betting we can make the jump back and still head home when we want to. In fact, I might be ready to do a little more jumping around instead of flying in a straight line all the time."

"I think I agree with you, Bridget," Barnaby concluded. "I'll set the tempometer for 1903, and let's see what happens."

CLICK! HUMMM! Everything went smoothly, except they all felt that the trip took longer than it should have. Beauregard decided he'd better have a look at the tempometer before anyone stepped outside. To his horror, he saw that they had gone back to 1903 B.C.! He turned to his comrades.

"We do appear to have a small problem, actually," he began. "I think you might be surprised to know that you are more likely to watch a pyramid being built than to witness the Wright brothers fly. We've gone back just a little too far!"

"No worries," Barnaby said. "We accidentally flipped this B.C./A.D. switch over here. I'll just click it back to the A.D. position and we'll be on our way."

"Hey! Not so fast! Don't we at least want to take a look outside?" Bridget said excitedly. "Who knows what we might see!"

"Maybe we could save Ancient Egypt for another trip," Babette suggested. "I would love to see the great pyramids but for now, I would like to concentrate on American history. I would like to get a little closer to home, too, I think."

"I see your point," Bridget conceded. "Let's head toward home then."

This time, Beauregard checked the settings and threw the switch, just to make sure that his human friends didn't make another mistake.

The travelers looked out at a fantastic scene. They had landed on the Outer Banks of North Carolina, a great stretch of land and sand that juts out into the Atlantic Ocean. In the distance, the ocean glistened in the sunlight, but that didn't mean it was warm. The ocean breeze was stiff, and there was a brisk December nip in the air. They were surrounded by sand dunes, some almost as tall as *Lady Liberty*, but they could still see the hills behind them.

"We've got to get up to Kill Devil Hills," Barnaby said, pointing the way. "The Wright brothers flew their plane from there."

It took the travelers quite a while to cover the distance from the dunes to the hills. The walk was worth it though, because the first thing they heard as they reached the hilltop was the whirring sound of a small engine. In fact, it was a *very* small engine—almost too quiet. But there on the hilltop, Orville and Wilbur Wright were ready to fly. The travelers sat down on the edge of the field to watch the proceedings.

"We're here! We're really right here at this critical moment in the twentieth century," Barnaby said with great excitement. "Let's go over and meet them."

"I think we would be better to wait," Beauregard intervened. "Why don't we watch people fly for the first time and savor the moment? It will be an event we will always remember."

There was no disagreement, so they all settled down to watch the flight. Within minutes, the two-winged plane was on the move. It lifted off the ground, and landed again. There were four such flights that day in December, and the longest one lasted fifty-nine seconds, by Barnaby's watch.

"Well, that was hardly the most majestic event I've witnessed," Bridget said, disappointed. "I thought those guys really flew high in the air. It looked more like a puddle jump to me."

"But they do fly higher one day," Barnaby reminded her. "This is still a really important moment. This is controlled flight!"

"This has been quite an afternoon, I think," Babette said dreamily. "I know I will always remember this day as being very special."

"Please don't start getting sentimental on me, Frenchie," Bridget said. "After all, we haven't even met these guys yet."

"This might sound bizarre, but I think I am happy just watching them fly," Babette replied. "I do not think I really need to meet them in order to appreciate what they have accomplished. As Beauregard said, I am savoring the moment."

"Well, I guess you're right," Bridget admitted. "You know, there are a few African American inventors I would like to check out, but I'm also thinking I'd like to get back to see my parents."

"Which inventors are you talking about, Bridget?" Barnaby asked.

"Jan Matzeliger and Garrett Morgan," Bridget responded. "Matzeliger invented a machine that could make shoes in lots of different sizes. And Morgan developed the traffic light."

"I'd like to pay those guys a visit," Barnaby said.

"I agree," Babette said. "I'm ready for more."

"Well…would you guys mind if we take a little break from the time travel routine and check out my folks for a bit?" Bridget said hesitantly. "I'm not trying to be Captain Bringdown or anything, but we could all crash at my house for a while. You know, Mom and Dad have these cool clothes from the twenties and thirties. There are lots of trunks full of stuff we could investigate. Some old photo albums, too. What do you say?"

There was a short silence. Bridget wasn't sure what to think. Then, there was a loud chorus of agreement from her three companions. Bridget was really excited.

"New York City, here we come!" she sang.

The weary time travelers headed back to *Lady Liberty*. As they walked, Bridget smiled and said to her friends, "You know, Dorothy was right. There's no place like home."

✍ QUIZ #5 ✍
Machines!

1. Who invented the telephone?

2. Who invented the traffic light?

3. Who invented the light bulb?

4. Who created the conveyor belt?

5. Who were the first people to fly an airplane?

6. Who improved shoe manufacturing?

7. Who created the phonograph?

8. Who made automobiles at a price his own workers could afford?

9. Who was the Scottish immigrant who taught teachers of the deaf?

10. Who invented the "camera" that was the forerunner of the motion picture?

✍ **FOOD FOR THOUGHT** ✍

Here are a few questions that don't necessarily have one answer! Write your answers in your workbook, and write as much as you wish. Be sure to explain your responses.

1. If you decided to become an inventor, what inventions would you want to create? Why?

2. You read about some famous people and their inventions in this chapter. Which invention was the most important, in your estimation? Why?

3. If you could meet any inventor, who would it be? What questions would you ask him or her? (Don't limit yourself to those mentioned in this chapter!)

4. What are the qualities of the most successful inventors? Which quality do you think is the most important? Why?

✐ GROUP ACTIVITIES ✐

Do as many of these activities as you wish. Work in groups to accomplish these goals, and be sure to have fun!

1. Choose an inventor you admire. Gather information about the person's life and interests. Then, stage an interview: You be the inventor and have your group members interview you about your life.

    Take turns, with each member being a different inventor. The interviewers should try to guess the inventor's identity based on his or her responses.

2. Build a model, draw a picture, or create a story about your favorite invention. Share your model, drawing, or story with your friends and show them how the invention works!

3. Who was George B. Selden? How did he lose to Henry Ford? Who deserves credit for the invention? Why? Stage a skit in which Ford and Selden meet and debate the issue.

Chapter 7
The Roaring Twenties and the Depressing Thirties

1918 ▶ World War I ends

1920 ▶ Warren G. Harding elected president; Women vote for the first time

1921 ▶ Albert Einstein lectures at Columbia University

1923 ▶ President Harding dies; Calvin Coolidge becomes president; Teapot Dome Scandal uncovered

1925 ▶ John Thomas Scopes convicted for teaching evolution

1926 ▶ Gertrude Ederle becomes the first woman to swim the English Channel; National Broadcasting Company (NBC) founded

1927 ▶ Charles Lindbergh's solo flight of the Atlantic Ocean; Babe Ruth hits his 60th home run

1928 ▶ Walt Disney's "Steamboat Willie," the first cartoon to use sound, is produced; it stars Mickey Mouse

1929 ▶ Stock Market crashes on October 29th; Great Depression begins

1932 ▶ Franklin Delano Roosevelt elected president; Amelia Earhart becomes the first woman to fly the Atlantic alone

1933 ▶ Adolf Hitler becomes Chancellor of Germany

1939 ▶ World War II begins in Europe when Nazi Germany invades Poland; Gone with the Wind and Wizard of Oz released

I must say that I enjoyed meeting so many unusual minds. Of course, I was a little shocked at the crowd's reaction when I told that man not to be so rude! Imagine yelling derogatory comments like that about the feline community and thinking he could get away with it! He obviously needed a few lessons in mannerly conduct. I thought I straightened him out very politely, but that crowd just got hysterical. You know, humans would be very surprised indeed if they knew *all* the things we felines can do. But then, I digress...

I thought Bridget's idea of a trip home was splendid! After all, I'd been away for quite some time, so I was ready for a little relaxation. Why, I was just thinking about my lovely red tabby friend Tallulah when Bridget, Babette, and Barnaby decided to check out all the goodies in the attic. There were some rather distasteful items amongst the twenties clothing, but all the young people used to wear them, believe me. Can you imagine, for instance, wearing a raccoon coat? But that's not all! I was really surprised when those attic treasures got us into some big trouble...

✐ ✐ ✐ ✐ ✐

"**D**o you think your parents will mind if we visit for a few days?" Babette asked, as they floated above Bridget's neighborhood. "We did not really ask them, did we?"

"No problem," Bridget said as they had landed gracefully in her street. "When we got back to Dr. Tempus Fugit's laboratory, I called them and asked if it was all right for you guys to crash for a few days. Actually, they were really excited about it and asked what we'd like for dinner! They're really cool like that."

"Well, I can tell you that I'm looking forward to living in the present for a while," Barnaby said. "I think we deserve a rest!"

"I am so looking forward to seeing all those things your parents have stored in the attic. It will be just as if we are time traveling when we open up those trunks to see what is in them," Babette said excitedly.

"I never realized how exciting that old stuff could be," Bridget replied. "It's so long since I've looked at it that I can hardly remember what's there."

Bridget's mom appeared as the group reached the front door. "Bridget, how's my baby doing?" she said, giving Bridget a big hug.

Bridget's mom also hugged Babette and Barnaby, and Beauregard received an enthusiastic scratch behind the ears. "It's so nice to have you here. I don't think I've seen you since that time in Paris," she said. "We'll all have a nice dinner and sit around and chew the fat for a while. That will be so pleasant!"

A strange look came over Babette's face. "Excuse me, Bridget," she said quietly, "but please tell your mom to give my portion of fat to you. I really do not think I would enjoy chewing fat."

"Not again, Babette! Mom just means that we'll sit down and talk, not chew fat literally. It's just an old expression," Bridget laughed. A look of relief came across Babette's face.

Everybody moved into the living room where Bridget's dad gave the kids and the cat a warm greeting. They sat around having cool drinks and chips while dinner was cooking.

"Bridget says you have an attic full of interesting things from the twenties and thirties," Barnaby said. "Would you mind if we looked around up there? We're pretty interested in history right now."

Bridget's mother smiled. "Sounds like fun to me," she said. "But I'm not really sure what's up there. We inherited it from our parents, and we haven't been through it in years."

"Say, maybe you could do an inventory for us! You know, make a list of all the things you find," Bridget's dad said.

Bridget winced. "Sounds like work to me, Dad," she replied. "But I guess we could make it fun. Is that all right with you?" she asked the others.

"I'll use my clipboard," Barnaby said, as he pulled one from his unruly hairdo, complete with paper and pencil.

"I'll be happy to try on any clothing to check the sizes," Babette volunteered. "I would enjoy seeing the American styles of that period."

"Who are you kidding, Frenchie?" Bridget chuckled. "You're a clothing freak if ever I saw one. You love to try on stuff, so you're perfect for the job."

Bridget's mom and dad went to check on dinner, and a few minutes later they called everybody to the table for a wonderful feast—roast beef, mashed potatoes, green beans, salad, apple pie…yummmmm!

After dinner, everybody was so full that it felt like instant nap time. Resisting the urge to lie down on a full stomach, Bridget's dad began to reminisce about his childhood, and the stories his parents used to tell him about life in the twenties and thirties.

"My parents remembered that era with mixed feelings," he said. "The twenties were filled with many great achievements…the first transatlantic solo flight by Charles Lindbergh and several accomplishments by women like Gertrude Ederle, the first woman to swim the English Channel, and Amelia Earhart, the first woman to fly across the Atlantic. Most importantly, women's suffrage was achieved by people like Susan B. Anthony and Elizabeth Cady Stanton. There was a pervasive feeling, however, that people should take advantage of the moment because tomorrow may never come. Despite all the advances, it seemed like the Great War had destroyed people's faith in the future."

"I think you lost me," Barnaby interjected. "Which war was the 'Great War'? And why wouldn't people be happy once it was over?"

"Good questions, Barnaby!" Bridget's dad responded. "'The Great War' was the First World War, 'the war to end all wars,' the war fought 'to make the world safe for democracy.' Do you hear the idealism in those phrases? Well, the First World War taught Americans a bitter lesson—many, many people died, and many returned injured or permanently maimed. After that, Americans adopted a *carpe diem* attitude, a live-for-the-moment approach to life. And who could really blame them? The 1920s began to roar with a new lawlessness. Prohibition had been adopted as an amendment to the Constitution, outlawing the use of alcohol nationwide, but some people made great fortunes by smuggling or bootlegging homemade alcohol, selling it through illegal bars called speakeasies. Before the war got under way, Americans thought the world would be a better place after it was fought and won. After the war, they were not so optimistic."

"So they decided to party, is that it?" Bridget asked her father. "They thought that parties could help them forget their losses?"

"Yes, and make the most of the moment, since they were no longer sure how long it would last," Bridget's dad concluded.

"So that's why they call it the Roaring Twenties!" Barnaby said. "The speakeasies, the gangsters, the fads…some of that makes more sense now. But what about the thirties? Why did everything go from wild and crazy to depressing and gloomy?"

"Another good question, and a complex one, too," Bridget's dad replied. "You see, world economies were in turmoil following the war. The United States decided to isolate itself from world problems and build a tariff barrier so that foreign goods would be more expensive than American-made products. Foreign countries responded by putting similar tariffs on American products. The flow of resources and money among countries was very restricted. In America, credit spending became the rage and people bought up goods that they could not really afford. Eventually, this 'false economy' caused a worldwide depression. And the depression ultimately became the cause of another world war!"

"I must express some confusion here, too," Babette said. "I do not understand how tariffs work as barriers to trade among countries. What does trade have to do with the depression?"

"Hmmm. I said this was very complex," Bridget's dad replied. "Think of a tariff as a tax. If you were importing French products to America, the federal government would charge you a tax to sell your products here. So, the French products would cost more than their American competitors. The French government could retaliate by adding a tariff on American goods sold in France. Consumers in all countries would be looking for the best deals so naturally, they'd buy the cheaper, domestic products. A healthy economy depends on both foreign and domestic markets for buying and selling, but if everyone is buying domestic products on credit, no money is changing hands, just promises to pay. Money stopped circulating among countries and within countries. Ultimately, the American economy suffered massive unemployment, with over a third of the work force out of a job. Some people lost everything they had, including some of the very wealthy who had invested heavily in the stock market. When the stock market crashed on October 29, 1929, businesspeople and farmers alike were facing the worst financial crisis in American history!"

"This is such a depressing topic," Bridget said gloomily. "Now I know why people had such a difficult time during the thirties. Everyone had to work so hard just to survive. Didn't they have soup lines and bread lines where people could eat, too?"

"Yes, you're right, Bridget. There were soup kitchens where the homeless and unemployed could get a free meal," Bridget's father responded. "But don't be depressed altogether by the Great Depression! It was also an era in which people stuck together and helped each other out. Families lived in difficult conditions, but they learned the importance of working together to survive. It was a time when people learned to appreciate all the little things in life that they had previously taken for granted. In some ways, the thirties were a great antidote for the negativity of the twenties. I guess people figured out that life was worth living after all!"

"I think it's time for you young people to get a good night's sleep," Bridget's mom said. "I don't suppose anybody needs a snack before bed?"

Only Bridget's dad headed to the kitchen for a glass of milk before bed. "I'll see you tomorrow and we'll talk some more, if you like. Be careful with those old trunks in the attic. You never know what you might find."

When Bridget's mom and dad had gone to bed, Babette looked at her friends and said, "I enjoyed that conversation with your father very much, Bridget. How does he know so much about American history?"

Bridget smiled with pride. "Dad has always loved history. Those trunks full of stuff are part of our family's heritage. I bet he can't wait until we make an inventory of all the things we find up there. It's sort of like finding out about yourself by looking at the way your family used to live before you were born, you know?"

"You are absolutely right," Barnaby said. "I once found myself wanting to look through all the stuff in my family's attic, to see what I could learn about our past."

"Well, tomorrow morning, we'll start the inventory! Right now, I'm ready for bed. I'll see you to your rooms and sack out for a while." Bridget yawned and stretched.

When they awoke the next morning, there was breakfast waiting on the table, along with a note.

Be sure to have some breakfast before you begin work! We'll see you this evening when we get home. Call us at work if you need us. Have fun and be careful!

Love, Mom and Dad

The attic was full of trunks and racks of old clothing. Barnaby immediately took charge of the inventory procedure and they decided which trunk they would open first. Barnaby stood by, clipboard in hand, ready to write down everything they found.

Finally, the moment came to open the first trunk. Bridget carefully lifted the lid and peeked inside. She suddenly sneezed violently three times in a row! Then, a look of dismay crossed her face. The trunk was full of old photograph albums covered with dust. Bridget didn't look happy.

"Well, this is hardly what I'd call treasure," she said. "Let's try another one."

Before anyone could respond, she jumped to the next trunk to see what it contained. As she opened this one, a broad smile crept across her face. She flung the lid wide open to reveal an elaborate, folding mirror. Babette and Bridget carefully lifted their find from the trunk, set it up, and propped it against the wall. Barnaby began scribbling down a description: "One antique, folding, gilt-edged mirror, four feet tall..."

"Wow! That's a really cool mirror," Bridget exclaimed. "It looks like an antique to me."

"Oooh, it's perfect for trying on clothes," Babette cooed. "Why don't we try some things off the rack over there just to see how we look?"

"Now we don't want to be permanently distracted from our task," Barnaby cajoled.

But it was too late. Bridget and Babette had started to check out the old clothes. Babette found an old twenties dress and was trying it on with a matching hat. Soon she was wearing an entire flapper outfit, complete with spangles and bows. The hat looked something like a bell with a bow, and it completely covered her forehead. Bridget giggled at the sight, but by now she also looked pretty weird in a long, straight skirt and burgundy shoes with solid, curving heels.

Suddenly, Barnaby was also in action. He'd spotted an old fur coat that appeared to be made of raccoon. Within seconds, he was wearing it.

Meanwhile, Beauregard had finished the dishes. He took off his apron and rubber gloves, and sauntered upstairs to see what his friends had discovered. It was a bad moment. As he crested the attic stairs, he let out a mighty rowl of disapproval. There was Barnaby, prancing around in an oversized fur coat! Bridget, Babette, and Barnaby tittered nervously—they knew how upset that kind of stuff made Beauregard. They tried to placate him.

"Don't worry," Bridget soothed. "We're only trying these things on for fun! See? We're going to model them in front of this fantastic mirror we found. Come on you two, let's stand in front of the mirror together so we can check out how we'd look in the twenties! Beauregard, put on that hat and come join us."

The foursome gathered in front of the ornate mirror to see what they looked like and to laugh at their costumes. As they struck various poses, an unusual glow began to emanate from the mirror. Bridget noticed it first...

"Wow! This mirror is giving off some pretty strange vibes," she said suspiciously. "Do you think there's something wrong with the lights in here or is that mirror really beginning to glow?"

Those were her last words. As they gathered to peer into the mirror's surface, a vortex developed that sucked them instantly into another world, a world where their clothing looked like the chic fashion of the day.

"Wh—Where are we?" Bridget asked. "This street looks kind of familiar, but I just can't place it. Anybody have any ideas?"

"Judging from the height of the buildings and the climate, I'd say we're still in New York City!" Barnaby said excitedly. "I just don't know what time period we've hit. This raccoon coat feels more like it suits me, though. Maybe we're in the twenties!"

"Ah, Americans are sooo analytical," Babette said. "If the clothing fits, it does seem reasonable to assume that the mirror tailored the situation to our style of dress. So, I think you are correct, Barnaby. We are somewhere in the twenties. But how could such a mirror exist?"

"I've got an idea!" said Bridget suddenly. "I wonder if Dr. Tempus Fugit is in the Statue of Liberty. Maybe we could find him and he could help us out of this mess. We've got to be home by dinnertime, or Mom and Dad will think we were kidnapped!"

"That's a good idea, assuming that all of our previous assumptions are correct," Barnaby said. "Why don't we get an aerial view of the city and see if we can find the Statue of Liberty? We'll try to find our way once we're airborne."

Bridget had already started to inflate one of her famous bubble balloons for the trip. It was a beautiful crisp day with a slight breeze, and they began a rather steep ascent to see if they could figure out exactly where they were. Bridget had to make some adjustments to the size of the balloon to account for the extra weight of the raccoon coat, which seemed to weigh a ton. When they had reached a decent altitude, Barnaby began to spot landmarks, but how different they looked!

"That looks like Ellis Island over there—the place where all the immigrants first landed when they came to America. And look, there's the Statue of Liberty over there. We're in New York City, but there are hardly any tall buildings! Babette, you're right. We're in the twenties!"

Bridget steered them toward the familiar Statue of Liberty and they landed without a problem on the shores of the famous island in New York Harbor. They headed toward the base of the statue, hoping to find Dr. Tempus Fugit and a solution to their dilemma. They made it inside, but Dr. Tempus was nowhere to be found. In frustration, Bridget decided to ask a guard standing nearby if he knew the good doctor.

"Er...a...excuse me, Sir, could you direct us to the laboratory of Dr. Tempus Fugit? We're old friends of his," she said tentatively.

"Senior or junior?" the guard asked affably. "They're both downstairs, but I'm afraid I'll have to see some sort of identification first."

"Just tell him that Beauregard and his friends are here to see him. That should be enough," Bridget responded confidently.

The guard disappeared into the depths of the statue's basement. He returned within a few minutes and smiled pleasantly. "The doctor will be with you shortly," he informed them.

When the doctor appeared, he was much younger than the time travelers had anticipated. His hair and mustache were just as unruly as ever, but they were dark brown and his stride was clearly not the characteristic shuffle they knew so well.

The doctor extended his hand and shook hands and paws all around. "Have we met before?" he inquired. "I have the strongest feeling that you are an important part of my future, for some reason."

Bridget, Babette, Barnaby, and Beauregard all looked at each other for just a moment. Then Barnaby ventured an explanation.

"Well, Sir, you might say that you have met us before, but not yet!" he said tactfully.

The young doctor's eyes widened, almost as if he had received an electric shock. His hair, of course, maintained that shocked look on a permanent basis, although the friends noted that it popped up another couple of inches. "You...you're from the future...my future," he said with a dazed look on his face. "Come with me," he said, and they all retreated to the basement laboratory. When they reached the lab, he seemed to have recovered from the initial shock of the encounter with his future.

"My father and I have been engaged in time travel research for five years, ever since Albert Einstein's lecture on the theory of relativity in April, 1921 in which he introduced time as the fourth dimension," Dr. Tempus Fugit said. "I will assume that our research is ultimately successful because all of you are here and because you came in search of me. But are you in some sort of trouble?" he inquired.

"Wow, Doc! You're one smart cookie to piece this situation together so quickly," Bridget responded. "Yeah, we are in a bit of a jam. We were trying on these clothes in front of a beautiful mirror we found in my folks' attic. The mirror gave off this weird glow and we moved closer to investigate it. All of a sudden, we were transported to the twenties! We hope you can help us figure out how to get home."

"You must have crossed a time threshold somehow," Dr. Tempus Fugit replied thoughtfully. "You will probably have to go back the same way. It is a dangerous gamble, but it really is your only hope."

"You don't mean that we are trapped here, do you?" Babette asked. "How are we to find such a threshold again?"

"We aren't certain how they open or even when they will open next," Dr. Tempus replied thoughtfully. "We will need to return to your point of entry and wait for the threshold to reappear. Come, we should be on our way."

"Wait! Can't we look around a little on our way? We don't even know what year we're in or what's going on," Bridget said excitedly. "Why don't you tell us what's happening?"

Dr. Tempus Fugit smiled. "Well, I guess if I were in your shoes, I'd want to know more, too. I might even have a few questions for you." The young doctor relaxed into his chair and gestured to the others to sit down also. Then he began to reflect about the last few years of life in America.

"Let's see. Where to begin...Well, Warren G. Harding was elected president in 1920 but died in office in August, 1923. His administration was troubled by the revelation of the Teapot Dome scandal, and many believe that he died before the public was informed and his reputation ruined. His Secretary of the Interior, Albert B. Fall, illegally leased naval oil reserves in Teapot Dome, Wyoming to Mammoth Oil Company, which was controlled by Harry F. Sinclair. Harding was a man who trusted his friends, but his friends turned out to be his worst nightmare. His vice president, Calvin Coolidge, completed Harding's term and is the current president. He really believes that a 'government which governs least, governs best.' I guess that means that the government ought to stay out of the way of business and let the economy regulate itself. I just wonder how all of this credit spending and stock market speculation is really going to affect us in the long run, though. The country is experiencing widespread prosperity here in 1927. The National Broadcasting Company, the first nationwide radio broadcasting network, started in 1926. And a man named Charles Lindbergh is about to attempt to fly the Atlantic alone from New York to Paris. Prohibition has produced all kinds of problems like bootlegging and smuggling illegal whiskey; illegal bars called speakeasies are all over the city, and lots of organized crime has developed, along with the prosperity."

The young doctor stopped his reflections for a moment and chuckled, "But you already know all this, don't you? And you must know how all of these situations turn out."

"We know how some events turn out, that is true," Babette said calmly. "But we dare not break the rule you taught us before we left the first time: Don't tamper with the future by influencing past events. We might change the course of history if we told you what we know."

"I taught you that rule?" Dr. Tempus Fugit said excitedly. "So I am responsible for your initial time travel adventures? Well then, I must continue my research! But come, we must get you back through the mirror before the opportunity disappears. Remember, I am not certain that you will return to the same location. You may arrive in another year, so be very careful. Return to your entry point and wait for the time portal to open again, if you don't find yourselves at home. Let's go."

"We'll be going through the city to my neighborhood, Dr. Tempus," Bridget said. "Maybe we can take in a few sights on the way!"

"Please, there is some urgency here," Dr. Tempus warned. "If you miss the opportunity to return, you may be here for quite some time. We'll take the ferry to Manhattan and hire a cab to take us to your neighborhood."

The ferry departed and everyone enjoyed the opportunity to relax. It really was a beautiful day. When they docked, Dr. Tempus Fugit hailed a cab and they began the dash to Bridget's home. They reminisced about their visit with Henry Ford as they drove along in a 1927 Ford through congested streets filled with the sound of beeping horns and the smell of car exhaust. Everyone seemed to be moving at a frantic pace.

Suddenly, they found themselves in the middle of a large traffic jam. Horns were beeping wildly, but no one was going anywhere.

"What's takin' so long?" the cabbie kept asking. He was getting more frustrated by the minute.

Barnaby nudged Bridget. "Why don't we get out and walk around the jam? Maybe we can pick up another cab on the other side of this mess."

"That sounds like a good idea to me," Bridget answered. "Come on, folks. Let's walk."

Dr. Tempus paid the cabbie, who was not at all happy about losing part of his fare, but the traffic remained at a standstill as the group headed down the street on foot. They walked in the direction of the confusion, hoping to find out what was going on. By now, night was beginning to fall.

"Look over there," Babette pointed. "There are some police cars blocking off the street. What could be going on? A celebrity of some sort?"

"I think we should investigate," Barnaby said. "It could be important."

As they approached, a policeman shouted a warning. "Please stay away from this area. We suspect illegal alcohol is being sold in this building and we're going to raid the establishment!"

"Let's slip down this alley and see if we can catch a glimpse of the place," Bridget suggested. "It would be cool to see what's going on in there."

"You're going to get us into trouble, Bridget," Babette warned. "Maybe we should just watch from the street."

Dr. Tempus intervened. "I agree with Babette, especially as we're pressed for time. We should be moving along."

"Just a quick peek!" Bridget pleaded. "Then we'll go!"

The group headed down the alley, and waited for a chance to check out what was going on inside the building. Just as they reached a heavy-looking door, a pretty tough character emerged from it.

"This ain't no place for kids, see?" the man said. "So why don't you go back the way you came! Now!"

"Why, you must be a mindreader! That is precisely what we're attempting to do!" Beauregard was displeased with the man's rudeness, and was about to tell him so.

Babette stepped back from the others and started making strange sounds, ready to spring into action. Bridget, Barnaby, and Dr. Tempus were still recovering from the man's verbal assault.

"My friends and I were merely curious to see what was going on behind that big green door," Beauregard continued. "Do you think you could show us around?"

The man's face turned beet red. Suddenly, he reached into his pocket. Babette dropped into the classic karate pose, ready to attack. The entire group jumped back, preparing for the worst. The man produced a badge.

"I am an undercover agent with the Treasury Department. We're here to bust this place for selling illegal alcoholic beverages. If you step one foot or paw in this place, I'll arrest you along with the rest of the clientele in that sleazy establishment," he announced sternly.

"But officer, we're only curious bystanders," Bridget replied. "We just want to see what it's like in there. Couldn't you take us inside for just five minutes? We'll leave before you guys bust the joint, okay?"

"Well…okay. I'll let you inside for a couple of minutes. But stay close to the door! I'll get in big trouble if anything goes wrong in there, so look around fast, then leave."

The undercover cop rapped three times on the big green door. A small peep hole opened and a voice said, "What's the password?"

"Charleston," the officer replied.

As they went through the door, Babette asked, "That is a city in South Carolina, yes? Why would they use it for a password?"

Beauregard quickly explained. "It's a popular dance they're talking about, not the city. You'll see."

Once inside, the time travelers caught sight of the dance floor. The phonograph was cranking out some tunes at high volume. A guy with a megaphone was urging couples onto the dance floor, and the rhythm was infectious. The couples were facing each other, stepping and kicking with wild abandon.

"What's the dance they're doing?" Bridget asked the officer.

"You must be from the country," the officer laughed. "Don't you recognize the Charleston when you see it?"

"I'm from New York City, sir!" Bridget responded briskly. "Come on you guys, let's show the officer that we can do the Charleston!"

Bridget and Beauregard, Barnaby and Babette headed to the dance floor, leaving Dr. Tempus Fugit with the undercover agent.

The foursome picked up the dance by following the wild variations they saw all around them. They were kicking high and stepping low, crossing their knees, and trucking with the best of them.

Suddenly, the man with the megaphone made a startling announcement. "Ladies and gentlemen, this is a RAID!"

Pandemonium broke loose! People were running in every direction. Policemen were pouring in from every direction. The time travelers fled the dance floor, searching desperately for the door.

"Over here, over here!" Dr. Tempus was gesturing wildly. "We can leave through this door. Follow me!"

The group followed Dr. Tempus down a narrow passageway that came up through a utility hole in the middle of a street over a block away. Fortunately, the traffic was light, and they crawled out of the hole without much difficulty.

"Whew!" Bridget said, wiping her forehead. "That was a close call."

"We've lost valuable time," Barnaby interjected. "It's already dark. Should we find a place to sleep for the night or should we still try to find the time portal?"

"I'm afraid we must push on," Dr. Tempus said. "Come, let's resume our trip by cab. There may still be a chance to get you home tonight."

As they got into the cab, weary from their recent escapades, Babette was still talking about the Charleston. "I don't believe I have ever seen such an energetic dance. Where do they get all that energy?"

"Remember what Dad was saying?" Bridget answered. "Every-body got into wild living to make the most of the present. I guess dances and fads help us get a feel for people's attitudes toward life. Know what I mean?"

"We're here," Dr. Tempus Fugit announced. "This is the address you gave me."

Dr. Tempus paid the cab driver, and the group was left in the dark residential neighborhood. It was a beautiful warm evening, and a canopy of stars was clearly visible. They all sat down in a circle on the ground, and waited for something to happen. In the meantime, they reflected about the day's events and about life in the twenties.

"It looks like the police are having a difficult time enforcing prohibition, judging from the crowd in that speakeasy," Babette said. "Do you think gangsters are involved?"

"Well, underworld figures like Al Capone are making a fortune by breaking the law, and lots of people admire them for it," Dr. Tempus replied. "I think he is a very dangerous, violent man. I'm sure he must be involved in all kinds of illegal activities."

"It's interesting to reflect about people and their heroes," Barnaby said. "Some people idolize sports figures like Babe Ruth and Lou Gehrig. Others think gangsters are heroes because they beat the system."

"Well, I think of people as heroes when they have the courage to make difficult choices, despite the odds," Bridget added. "I guess Lindbergh is a hero because he's going to fly 3,600 miles across the Atlantic in a single-engine plane, and so is Amelia Earhart because she will be the first woman to fly across the Atlantic. Those people have a lot of guts! I don't admire people who get ahead at other people's expense."

"I agree with you, Bridget," Barnaby replied. "I don't think violence should earn our admiration."

"One of my heroes is a high school teacher in Tennessee who decided to challenge a state law that made it illegal to teach about evolution," Dr. Tempus Fugit interjected. "Have you every heard of John Thomas Scopes? He is a hero to me because he stood up for his intellectual convictions."

Before anyone had the chance to respond, the huge oak tree in Bridget's front yard was surrounded by an eerie glow. Bridget stood up quickly and pointed toward the light.

"There's a tree house in that old oak tree. My dad and his friends used to tell stories about how the tree was haunted and stuff. Do you think…?" Her voice trailed off. The glow was growing brighter.

"You must go immediately, my friends. I cannot go with you. I will see you again very soon." Dr. Tempus Fugit knew that his life would never be the same after this strange encounter with people from his own future. "Don't be afraid! Safe home!" he called after them.

Bridget, Barnaby, Babette, and Beauregard scrambled up the trunk of the old oak and entered the tree house, now aglow with a light emanating from an empty picture frame that hung on the wall.

"We should move toward the frame and hope we make the trip back home," Bridget said. "Do you think this is what Dorothy felt like with the ruby slippers and everything?"

The light grew even brighter as they approached it. When it subsided, they were gone.

The time travelers found themselves sitting in a circle in the tree house. It was daylight.

"It didn't work," Bridget cried. "We're still here. How are we going to get back to the present?"

"Don't jump to conclusions," Barnaby said. "Let's see if we can figure out how far along the time line we've actually traveled."

Bridget spotted a woman entering the yard below. "That's not my mom! It looks like my grandmother, only about forty years younger. We're not home yet!"

"You are most certainly home," Babette consoled. "We're just a few years early, that's all."

"Let's get down out of this tree and do some exploring," Barnaby said. "We can't sit here all day waiting for the next launch window to occur."

"Well, I guess you're right," said Bridget sadly. "I just wanted to get home soon. We might as well find out what's going on. That was cool seeing Grandmom looking so youthful. I guess I'd better not introduce myself, huh?"

The time travelers stood up in order to make their way back down the tree. They noticed that their outfits had all changed to conservative thirties styles—no more raccoon coats and flapper dresses.

The first thing they heard when they descended from the tree was a song coming from a nearby phonograph or radio. Judging by the lyrics, the song's title was "Brother, Can You Spare a Dime?"

"I conclude that we're in the middle of the Great Depression," Barnaby said.

They sat down on the street corner, wondering what to do next. It wasn't an easy decision.

"I remember Dad talking about the massive unemployment during this time, and people having to wait in line for free food because they couldn't afford to buy any," Bridget said. "But I'm still not clear how all this depression stuff got started."

"Maybe I can help," Beauregard volunteered. "The term 'depression' used in this context doesn't refer to a collective bad hair day, that's for sure. It has to do with that stock market crash your father was talking about. Remember he said it occurred in October 1929? In more prosperous times, people bought stocks with borrowed money. Banks even bought stocks with people's savings. When the stock market crashed, people and banks sold their stocks for much less than they paid. So, millions of dollars were lost. But that wasn't all. Farmers were growing more crops than they could sell, but it cost them more to plant crops than they could earn from selling them. So, many farmers were losing their farms. And in the cities, factories were overproducing, but workers weren't even paid enough to buy the products they were making. So, factories closed, and more and more people became unemployed. Your father was right when he said that money stopped circulating throughout the economy. The government had to create jobs to get people back to work."

"Oh, I see now," Bridget replied. "But how did the country get out of such a mess?"

"I think World War II finally brought the country out of the Great Depression," Beauregard replied. "The New Deal programs were largely responsible for restoring faith in the economy and for getting people back to work."

"The New Deal? Where have I heard that term before?" Babette pondered. "It sounds almost like a game show on television."

"Well, Franklin D. Roosevelt *was* the first president to appear on television, but he was never on a game show," Beauregard laughed. "Roosevelt was elected president in 1932, beating the incumbent president, Herbert Hoover. Roosevelt created government jobs for the unemployed, establishing huge programs like the Civilian Conservation Corps and the Works Progress Administration to do things like build roads and bridges, government buildings and schools, and create national parks. He also subsidized farmers so that they got paid to grow less food. In this way, farmers could keep their farms and prosper, especially when food prices started to go up. Roosevelt's New Deal policies restored people's faith in government because they gradually worked to put people back to work, and money started to circulate again."

"Wow!" said Bridget. "That was impressive, Beauregard."

"I'm a bit of a history buff myself," the cat said modestly.

"You know, maybe we should go downtown and help out somehow, since we're here for the day. There must be something we could do," said Bridget.

"That's an excellent idea, Bridget," Babette responded. "It would be a good use of our time."

"I agree," said Barnaby. "We really need to be doing something useful during these hard times."

Bridget wasted no time. She blew another huge bubble balloon, and one by one, they jumped aboard for the ride downtown. The scene was quite different from the twenties. There were lots of people roaming the streets, including many children, with little or nothing to do.

Bridget, Babette, Barnaby, and Beauregard made their way through a long line of people and found themselves in the middle of a soup kitchen preparing to open its doors for lunch.

"We'd like to volunteer to help out," Barnaby called out.

About three voices answered simultaneously, "Yes!"

Then a woman came out from behind the counter and gave them each an apron to put on. By the time the soup kitchen doors were opened a few minutes later, each of the time travelers had been assigned the task of either preparing or serving the food. People lined up for a bowl of soup and a piece of bread. For some, it would be their only meal of the day. By the time the soup kitchen closed, the group was exhausted.

"I do not think I will ever forget the experience of serving so many people food," Babette said. "It reminds me of stories I have heard about life in Europe after the Second World War."

"I'll never complain about food again, I'll tell you that!" Bridget announced. "I'm glad we did it, though. It felt good to help out."

"Beauregard, were there any happy moments in the thirties?" Barnaby inquired. "I know things got slowly better, but were there any bright moments that people really enjoyed?"

"Well, I guess there were quite a few firsts in the movie world," Beauregard began. "In 1939, the movie version of Margaret Mitchell's novel, *Gone With the Wind*, was released. And how many times does one of us mention Dorothy or her famous ruby slippers? That same year, *The Wizard of Oz* was also released. Walt Disney's *Snow White and the Seven Dwarfs* was the top moneymaker of 1938. And Disney won an Oscar in 1933 for his cartoon *The Three Little Pigs*. And let's not forget that Mickey Mouse starred in the first animated cartoon to use sound, *Steamboat Willie*, way back in 1928! The motion picture industry as a form of entertainment must have helped to distract Americans from many of their hardships, don't you think?"

"Certainly," Babette replied. "But Americans also must have listened to the radio at home and been concerned about the rising tide of fascism throughout Europe. After all, Hitler invaded Poland in September, 1939, although he had become Chancellor of Germany much earlier, in 1933."

"I guess it's time to investigate the world wars," Barnaby said. "I suppose the turmoil in Europe must have occupied President Roosevelt's attention almost as much as the unemployment problems at home."

"I don't know about the rest of you guys," Bridget said abruptly, "but I need to get home. The last thing Mom and Dad would understand is my magical disappearance from the family attic. Know what I mean?"

The bubble balloon left the city for Bridget's neighborhood not long after Bridget's declaration of intent to return home. They arrived back in her neighborhood at dusk and quickly retreated to the confines of the tree house. There they waited patiently in a circle for the eerie glow to return. As they waited, they talked more about their recent experiences in the twenties and thirties.

Half an hour or so passed before the frame on the wall began its ritual, and the foursome moved toward it, waiting to be transported back to the present.

This time, the time travelers appeared in front of the mirror in Bridget's attic in the exact poses they had struck originally. They laughed and danced the Charleston in celebration, Babette swinging the strands of beads around her neck like the women in the twenties speakeasy. It was quite a celebration.

Then there came a deep voice from the foot of the attic staircase. "Hey, what's going on up there? Your mother and I have just gotten home and we'll have dinner ready in exactly one hour. So get things put away and get cleaned up for dinner. I'm looking forward to seeing the inventory you've made! Oh yeah, what did you think of that beautiful mirror? Pretty special, huh?

"Yeah, Dad," Bridget called back. "It's a very special mirror, that's for sure!"

✍ QUIZ #6 ✑
The Roaring Twenties and the Depressing Thirties

1. Who was the first woman to swim the English Channel?

2. When immigrants came to New York City, where did they first land in order to be admitted to the United States?

3. Who was president when the Teapot Dome scandal erupted?

4. Who was the first person to fly a transatlantic solo flight from New York to Paris?

5. Who was the first woman to fly across the Atlantic Ocean?

6. Who was the school teacher who challenged a Tennessee law that made it illegal for him to teach the theory of evolution?

7. Which president offered Americans a New Deal?

8. On what date did businesspeople and farmers have to face the worst financial crisis in American history?

9. Who proposed time as the fourth dimension in a lecture in New York City in 1921?

10. Who created the first animated cartoon to use sound, *Steamboat Willie*, in 1928?

✍ FOOD FOR THOUGHT ✍

This chapter offered some thoughts about life in the twenties and thirties. In your workbook, respond to any of the following questions. There are many possible answers, so look for evidence to support your thinking. Librarians, teachers, and parents can help you research any special interests you may have. Enjoy!

1. Who are your heroes? Why? Looking at the people you have chosen, write your own definition of the word "hero." Compare your definition with a friend's interpretation and talk about the similarities and differences.

2. There were lots of possible causes for the Great Depression—tariffs, stock market speculation, overproduction of crops and goods, low wages. Write your own explanation of how the Great Depression occurred. In your estimation, what factors contributed most to this crisis?

3. What does the term *carpe diem* mean to you? What are the strengths and weaknesses of this approach to living? How do you think it influenced people's lives in the twenties? And in the thirties?

4. What do you think of Calvin Coolidge's approach to government, typified by the sentence, "That government which governs least, governs best." Are there any modern day proponents of this idea? Who are they?

5. Prohibition made it illegal to consume alcoholic beverages. How did this law become an amendment to the Constitution of the United States? Why was it eventually repealed?

✍ **GROUP ACTIVITIES** ✍

Here are a few ideas for group activities that you can do with people who are interested in pursuing the same subject. Choose one and work together as a team to reach your goal. Be sure to have fun along the way!

1. Each member of your group should interview at least one person who lived through the Great Depression. Before you conduct the interview, each group member should agree on a set of questions to ask. After the interviews are done, see how the responses compare. Then, using what you learned from the interviews, write a short story, draw a picture, create a play, or write a song that expresses your results.

2. Research the clothing styles and fads of the 1920s. What did the clothing look like? Create your own twenties outfits! Use them to stage a fashion show for your families and friends. You could also create and perform a play or skit about the twenties and use the clothing as costumes for the production. Use a video camera to make a movie, if you prefer!

3. Some people believe that Roosevelt's New Deal polices began an era in which people began to look to the federal government to solve all of society's problems. Other people claim that Roosevelt's approach was the best way to get Americans back to work and restore faith in the national economy. What do you think about Roosevelt's New Deal? Stage a debate about the strengths and weaknesses of the New Deal approach. Be sure to use evidence to support your arguments.

Chapter 8
War and Peace: The Forties and Fifties

1914	Archduke Ferdinand assassinated; World War I begins
1915	*Lusitania* sunk by German U-boat
1917	United States enters World War I
1918	World War I armistice signed and hostilities end
1920	Prohibition (Eighteenth Amendment) goes into effect in the U.S.
1932	Franklin D. Roosevelt elected president
1933	Hitler becomes Chancellor of Germany
1939	World War II begins in Europe
1941	U.S. enters World War II when Japan attacks Pearl Harbor, December 7th
1942	Allies invade North Africa
1944	Allied invasion of Normandy, June 6th
1945	Franklin D. Roosevelt dies and Truman becomes president; Atomic bombs dropped on Japan; World War II ends; United Nations founded
1952	Eisenhower becomes president
1953	Joseph Stalin dies

Well, I can't imagine any more time traveling via magic mirrors! Give me the comforts of *Lady Liberty* any day! It was enjoyable watching my human friends dress up in the styles of the time, but I'm hoping that the human proclivity for fur will diminish as time goes by. And it is going by, isn't it? I never did get a chance to visit Tallulah with that mirror catching us all off guard. Maybe I'll just look around Bridget's neighborhood for some feline companions. It never hurts to look around, you know!

Speaking of looking around, Bridget's dad has certainly been very supportive of our attic investigations. I have a strange feeling that he knew about the mirror and the tree house. Anyway, there are some superb photo albums in those trunks that I'd love to examine more closely. Photographs can be so interesting! Why, I have a few albums of my own that I treasure as family keepsakes, mainly because they detail my own adventures with the feline community. Come to think of it, I need a photo of Tallulah and me for that collection. But I digress…

Do you know how to jitterbug? Ever heard of Bill Haley and His Comets? I'd have to answer "no" to both questions. Those high school kids we met from the fifties really did make us feel comfortable in their school. I never realized how the world wars influenced young humans during that period. I guess that living through a war really changes the way you view the future! Well, I hear Bridget's dad calling us for dinner again. I wonder if they would like my recipe for Mouseburger Helper…

✎ ✎ ✎ ✎ ✎

"Dad, some of those old trunks are filled with photos from the Second World War and the fifties," Bridget said, after an excellent evening meal. "I'm not sure what all that war stuff was about but it looked pretty interesting."

"In France, World Wars I and II evoke so many bad memories, so many hardships that I think it must be hard for many Americans to understand," Babette commented. "These wars…they were so devastating for Europe. How did America ever get involved in such horrible situations?"

"I've thought about the wars, too," Barnaby interjected. "I always wonder if all that incredible horror could have been avoided."

"You're offering some very interesting perspectives on the wars," Bridget's dad replied. "I'm not sure that I can answer all of your questions, but I'll try to help you out. Those old photographs can help to make some of my memories come alive by depicting something of what life was like during those times. Take a look through them when you get the chance." He turned to Babette. "The answer to your question is long and complicated. I'll try to explain, if you'll bear with me. Just interrupt if you have questions.

"If you want to understand World War II, you must first understand a few things about World War I. Remember when we were discussing the twenties and I told you that many Americans thought the First World War was the war to end all wars? I told you that the First World War changed America's attitude toward involvement in European affairs. Well, there's a reason for that! World War I broke out in Europe in 1914 and hostilities did not cease until November 11, 1918."

"How did the war start in the first place?" Bridget asked. "Didn't people know that violence never solves problems? It only makes things worse."

"I'm afraid that human beings have not given up using violent means to try to settle disputes, even today, after all kinds of wars have been fought. Look at the terrorist activities in the Middle East or the war in Bosnia, for example. They are born of ancient hatreds that are very hard to understand. The Bosnian situation actually involves some of the same basic problems that caused World War I to erupt in 1914. Archduke Francis Ferdinand was visiting Sarajevo, Bosnia when he was assassinated, setting off a powder keg that would take years to extinguish. There were two sets of alliances, the Triple Entente consisting of Great Britain, France, and Russia, and the Triple Alliance consisting of Germany, Austria-Hungary, and Italy."

"What do you mean, 'Austria-Hungary?'" Babette asked. "They are two separate countries."

"Well, today they are, but back then they were combined into one country containing German, Slavic, and Magyar peoples. It was a weak country troubled by continuing problems between the two groups. That's why the archduke was in Sarajevo. He thought he had a solution to all the ethnic troubles and was there to offer a remedy that would extend rights to the Slavic peoples within Austria-Hungary. The Austrian archduke's assassination set off the alliances and, one by one, the opposing sides declared war on one another. The war dragged on for years before the United States got involved. There were huge networks of trenches with barbed wire stretched between the opposing sides. They called the area between the trenches 'no-man's-land' because anyone caught out there would almost certainly be killed."

"How did the United States finally get involved?" Barnaby asked. "Did we try to break the stalemate?"

"Well, actually, the Germans had developed the submarine, nicknamed the U-boat, during World War I, and they began to practice unrestricted submarine warfare in the Atlantic, sinking the British ocean liner *Lusitania* in 1915 with one hundred Americans aboard. President Woodrow Wilson protested the action and the Germans promised not to attack any more commercial ships. Well, the British fleet's dominance of the high seas had to be broken, in Germany's estimation. The Germans decided to build a larger submarine fleet and resume unrestricted submarine warfare. When they announced their intentions publicly in January 1917, Wilson knew that the United States would be drawn into the war. The United States had been selling huge quantities of raw materials to Great Britain and its allies for the war effort, and there were huge loans to be repaid. So, it wasn't surprising that the United States decided to declare war on Germany in April 1917. The United States tipped the balance in the stalemate and, to make a long story short, an armistice was signed on the eleventh hour of the eleventh day of the eleventh month of 1918, with the peace treaty to be negotiated later."

"That is really quite a story, Dad," Bridget said. "But I don't see what the First World War has to do with the Second World War. Hadn't people had enough war?"

"I'm getting to that story right now, Bridget," her dad replied. "You remember that Woodrow Wilson was being extremely optimistic when he suggested that the First World War was 'the war to end all wars?' Wilson had proposed 'Fourteen Points' for a just and lasting peace in the world. He wanted those points incorporated into the Treaty of Versailles, which formally ended the war. The treaty, however, turned out to be a mixed bag. Great Britain and France wanted Germany to pay heavy war damages called reparations, and they succeeded in getting the treaty to make those claims against Germany. In return for giving in to those demands, Wilson got the Allies to agree to form a League of Nations. Wilson thought the League of Nations would solve future disputes before countries resorted to war. Instead, the League turned out to be a very weak organization without any real power to enforce its decrees. On top of that, Wilson couldn't get Congress to ratify the treaty because the United States turned isolationist and wanted nothing more to do with European affairs, as you might remember from our discussions about the twenties. So, the United States never joined the League of Nations! The Treaty of Versailles created a new democratic republic for Germany called the Weimar Republic, but the government was not able to deal with all the economic problems created by the war reparations payments and high inflation. The Treaty of Versailles was harsh in some respects and very lenient in others. When Adolph Hitler started his propaganda machine, he used the Treaty of Versailles as ammunition to convince the German people that they had been treated unfairly by the Allies. By the time he was appointed Chancellor of Germany in 1933, Hitler was planning to wage wars against all of Germany's old enemies, claiming that much of the land taken from Germany should be annexed or taken back by force. So the treaty became a tool for a fascist dictator like Hitler to convince his own people of some big lies that he created. He believed that people would believe big lies more easily than small ones. For instance, he manufactured the myth that German-speaking peoples were part of a superior race of beings who were destined to rule the world and used the idea to annex any German-speaking country to Germany. He started that process as early as 1936! He also blamed most of the financial problems on an international conspiracy of Jewish people, claiming that the Jews were responsible for all Germany's problems. I'm sure you remember that this kind of lie resulted in the murder of over six million Jews from all over Europe in concentration camps like Auschwitz and Dachau. There's much more to tell, but perhaps you have some questions?"

"You used the term 'fascist' a few times," Barnaby said. "Does fascism mean that a dictator rules the country?"

"Yes, but it also means having a strong belief in the importance of the nation, rather than in its individual citizens," Bridget's dad responded. "Remember how the Bill of Rights guarantees Americans certain individual freedoms? Well, fascist governments believe that their citizens have no rights. People exist to serve the nation. So, in fascist countries like Germany, Italy, and Japan during World War II, the people had to obey the rules established by dictators like Hitler, Mussolini, and Tojo, or face imprisonment, torture, or death. Fascist dictatorships also have this fanatical commitment to violence. They think war is the way to achieve cultural superiority and dominance over the world."

"So these fascist dictators were out to conquer the world?" Bridget asked. "Isn't that pretty ambitious?"

"But they almost succeeded," Babette said suddenly. "Hitler's armies swallowed almost all of the countries in Europe and France was occupied by the Nazis for over four years!"

"You're right, Babette, fascist governments did conquer much of the planet," Bridget's dad responded. "But that's another story. Maybe you guys should get some rest. We can talk more tomorrow night, if you like. Take a look at some of those old photo albums. Flip through some of the pages and see if that doesn't help you get a better idea of what the wars were like."

On their way to bed, Bridget looked at Barnaby and Babette with a little gleam in her eye. She was up to something.

"I have a better idea," she said finally. "I think it's time to visit Dr. Tempus again! That way, we can get a first-hand look at the wars just by borrowing *Lady Liberty* for the day."

"I'm ready to hit the road," Barnaby said enthusiastically. "But do you think it will be safe enough for us to travel during wartime?"

"We will just have to ask Dr. Tempus Fugit about that," Babette said. "But then, Beauregard has managed to get us out of some pretty dangerous situations."

The next morning, breakfast was waiting for them, along with another note telling them to be careful in the attic. Bridget, however, was preparing to blow another huge balloon for the trip to Liberty

Island. The foursome loved sailing past the skyscrapers and into the clear blue sky. It never seemed to lose its magic.

Before they knew it, the kids and the cat were reunited with Dr. Tempus Fugit in his laboratory. They were full of questions, but the doctor had a few things to tell them first.

"I've made a few little improvements you might like try out this time around," he smiled. "For one thing, I've outfitted *Lady Liberty* with an automatic timer. You can determine how long you'd like to stay at a given destination, set the timer, and the ship will automatically bring you back when your time expires!"

"That sounds great to me," Bridget said excitedly. "What year shall we visit first?"

"Wait! Wait! There's more!" Dr. Tempus announced dramatically. "I have also developed what I call my 'fly-on-the-wall' switch. If you don't want to be seen, this invention acts as a cloaking device, allowing you to observe your surroundings without being detected. But you must take special care because both devices are still experimental. Just remember one important point about the relationship between the devices: You can set the timer without using the cloaking device for the ship, but you cannot use the cloaking device without the timer!"

"Incredibly creative!" Barnaby complimented the doctor. "We look forward to using both devices since we may be involved in wartime situations on this trip."

"Wartime?" Dr. Tempus said nervously. "Which war? Where? I'm not sure that visiting a war zone is a very smart idea."

"World Wars I and II, if we're fortunate. Won't the cloaking device keep us out of harm's way?" Barnaby asked. "We can also set the timer to make sure we don't stay in one place too long. Your new inventions will probably get thoroughly tested, and that should prove very useful for you."

"Spoken like a true scientist, my young friend!" Dr. Tempus laughed. "All right. I'll go along with your decision, but you must be very careful with the technology you have at your disposal. If this time machine falls into the hands of any of the fascist dictatorships, it may mean the destruction of civilization as we know it. Are you prepared for that challenge?"

"I am prepared to fight to the death," Babette said emphatically. "The fascists will never be able to get this technology from me or my friends."

She sounded very serious. Dr. Tempus knew she meant business.

"You may be called on to fight if the fascists suspect anything whatsoever. The Nazis are very creative scientifically, and they would exploit any opportunity to discover the mysteries of time travel," Dr. Tempus stated. Then, he looked at his young friends and said, "You have much courage. Please select your destinations carefully and avoid battlegrounds. If *Lady Liberty* is damaged, you may never be able to return. Use the timer and the cloaking device as shields against harm. And get back here as soon as possible. I'll be worried until I see you return safely. Now, are you ready?"

The time travelers boarded their ship and discussed the best places to visit. They were nervous about the decision, but encouraged by the addition of two new devices that could help protect them from disaster.

"Where do we want to go?" Barnaby began. "What do we want to see? I'd be very interested in seeing the World War I battlegrounds but I'd like to avoid the fighting."

"Me, too," Bridget said. "Those trenches sound pretty incredible, but how do we see them while the war is going on?"

"That's simple," Babette said calmly. "Why don't we visit after the armistice was signed? That way we can see the trenches while avoiding the gunfire."

"Great idea, Babette," Bridget said. "Set the tempometer to November 11, 1918. We'll see what's happening on the western front."

Barnaby set the time indicator as Bridget had suggested. The primordial hum filled the cabin, the lights flickered, then everything went quiet.

"Quickly," Babette said urgently. "Use the cloaking device! If anyone sees us, we'll have a lot of questions to answer. Remember, we are in France. If anyone asks any questions, let me do the talking."

As they exited the time machine, the kids and the cat found themselves in the middle of "no-man's-land." Bridget almost stepped on a land mine but avoided disaster when Beauregard nudged her in a different direction. For miles around, all they could see were trenches, deep trenches where people could hide from withering machine gun fire, mustard gas, and land mines. The trenches were empty now, but just over the horizon, the sounds of celebration could be heard. And in English!

"It must be American soldiers from the American Expeditionary Force," Bridget said. "Remember Dad said that the Americans landed in 1918. Do you think we could talk to them?"

"We must be very careful where we walk," Babette said. "Look, there is a well-worn path to that trench. We should follow it to the voices."

Babette's plan worked. Within minutes, they were amongst the trenches. Then Barnaby, Babette, and Bridget thought they heard a small cough. They went over to the trench it appeared to be coming from, and looked down on Beauregard, who had donned a "doughboy" helmet. The trenches were ten feet deep in places, which greatly diminished Beauregard's size.

"Wow! Beauregard sure looks small in that trench," Bridget said. "It must have taken ages for it to get that deep! I wonder what they did when it rained?"

"I do not think they had much choice about what to do when it rained," Babette observed. "They must have stayed in the trenches for years, through all kinds of weather."

"Maybe we should ask the soldiers," Barnaby suggested. "But remember, the cloaking device uses a lot of energy, so we can't stay for long."

They helped Beauregard out of the trench and made their way along the path toward the sound of happy voices. Before long, they came across a couple of soldiers talking loudly about their futures.

"Well, I know I don't want to go back to farming when I return to Missouri," one of the soldiers said. "Why don't you and I start a men's clothing store in Kansas City when we get home? We could show them the latest styles *and* make a good living."

"That's a great idea, Harry!" the second soldier replied. "We could pool our money and join the business world."

Suddenly, both soldiers spotted the foursome coming through the trenches. They were quite surprised.

"I don't think I believe my eyes, Harry! That looks like three kids and a really big cat coming through the trenches." The soldier wore a look of total astonishment. "What do you make of it, Harry?"

"What brings you young folks and your cat to the trenches?" Harry asked as the time travelers approached. "The fighting is over and we're going home in just a few hours."

"We were curious about the trenches and the war," Babette said in her best French accent. "These trenches are so long and so deep that they must have been here for years. But how could anyone have fought in them for so long?"

"You can't be from the Meuse-Argonne area. But you're right, these trenches have been here for years," Harry replied. "I'm in artillery myself so I can't tell you from first-hand experience. But what my friends in the infantry tell me is that life was a living hell in these trenches. Floods, snow, ice…every person had to deal with the elements plus the mustard gas, artillery shells, and land mines. It was a nightmare. I figure the United States lost around a hundred thousand men, but altogether the Allies lost millions of men in these long, drawn-out campaigns. I sure hope that President Wilson was right when he said this was the 'the war to end all wars.'" As Harry described the horrors of the war, his initial happy demeanor changed to a much sadder, reflective one.

"I am sure that we French lost well over a million men in

this war," Babette said sadly. "It is such a horrible waste of life."

"War is never pretty," Harry replied. "But once it's started, somebody has to end it. I'm proud to say that the United States did its part to break the stalemate and bring the conflict to an end. Now, the peace treaty will be a different story…"

Barnaby began tugging on Babette's sleeve. He was pointing frantically at his watch.

Suddenly, the second soldier began pointing and jumping up and down, laughing wildly. "Look, Harry! Over there! Doesn't that look like the Statue of Liberty in the middle of no-man's-land?" He rubbed his eyes, as if he was seeing a mirage in the desert.

"Well, it sure looks like it!" Harry said. "C'mon, let's go take a look."

"Oh, ah…please excuse us now," Babette smiled apologetically. "We really must be leaving. We are quite late for a very important rendezvous. Good-bye! *Au revoir!*"

"Where's Beauregard?" Bridget whispered to Barnaby as they headed down the trench system with the soldiers right behind them.

"I have no idea," Barnaby said anxiously. "What a time for him to disappear! But if we don't beat these soldiers to the ship, we're going to have a lot of explaining to do!"

Suddenly, three beams of light shot out of *Lady Liberty*'s torch and Babette, Bridget, and Barnaby disappeared from the soldiers' view. Beauregard had remembered the teleportation device!

The three kids fell into a heap on the main cabin floor. Quickly, they scrambled to their seats and prepared for immediate departure. Beauregard had preset the tempometer at his own discretion. It read, "June 6, 1944."

"Did anybody catch the names on those soldiers' uniforms?" Bridget asked. "I know one was named Harry. Did you see his last name?"

"Yes, I did," Babette said. She looked at her friends and said, "Truman. Harry Truman." For just a few seconds, you could have heard a pin drop.

The hum began to grow, the lights flickered, and they left Harry

Truman and his friend somewhere in 1918. They were headed for D-Day and a glimpse of yet another world war. When all was quiet, nobody moved. Then, suddenly, Bridget jumped out of her seat and gave Beauregard a big hug.

"Thanks, Beauregard, for thinking ahead," she said. "You saved us again!"

Babette and Barnaby added their own hugs of appreciation, and Beauregard truly appreciated their gratitude.

When *Lady Liberty* made the jump, however, they had noticed that she seemed a little sluggish. A look of concern crossed Barnaby's face.

"We may have to monitor how much power these new devices drain from our reserves," he said, carefully studying the gauges. "In fact, I think we should stop for a more careful examination."

"If you think it's necessary," Bridget replied. "We don't want to be lost in the ozone for the rest of our lives!"

Babette almost asked Bridget what she was talking about, but instead she decided to look through the port hole to see where they had landed. Quickly, she snapped around in her chair and yelled a decisive command. "Engage the cloaking device immediately! We're in the middle of an airfield! There are biplanes all around us!"

Barnaby did not hesitate. He engaged the cloaking device, even though the power supplies seemed low. They couldn't risk being discovered.

In the meantime, Beauregard had popped the hatch and was preparing to disembark. To his left, he spotted an unoccupied biplane. He turned to his companions and said, "Now here's something I've always wanted to do! I'm headed for the cockpit of that biplane." The group scrambled after him.

"We have no idea where we are, and he's headed out to fly a biplane," Bridget moaned, as they walked onto the airfield.

"You know," Barnaby responded as they approached the plane, "I don't think we've gotten much past 1918, judging from this plane. It looks like we might have more problems with the time machine than I thought!"

By now, Beauregard had donned an aviator's cap and goggles, and was climbing into the cockpit to see for himself what it was like to be a World War I pilot. Just as he had settled down and was beginning to cruise the controls, he noticed a group of men headed toward the plane.

"I believe we have company," he called to his comrades. "I guess I'd better not try to crank the engine. They might think I'm trying to steal the plane."

Reluctantly, Beauregard popped out of the cockpit and landed on his two hind paws next to his friends. He did cut quite a dashing figure in his cap and goggles, but he left them in the biplane where they belonged.

"Well, that was a nice interlude! Shall we board our craft to avoid detection by those men who are now running across the field straight toward us?" Beauregard said.

The cloaking device made their first escape a bit tricky. In fact, Barnaby ran straight into *Lady Liberty*. "Ouch!" he cried, grabbing his head. Once the ship was located, however, they found that they had exited so many times that finding the hatch was easy. Safely inside, they decided to watch the results of their clever escape from the port hole. Barnaby rubbed his head, but he wasn't really hurt, since his hair had acted as a cushion.

"Those guys are in a panic to find us," Bridget observed. "They probably think we're spies or something."

The men were frantically searching the plane for evidence of the intruders but, of course, there was none to be found, except for a few black furballs.

"What language are they speaking?" Bridget said.

Babette and Barnaby listened intently. Suddenly, a very surprised look came across Babette's face.

"My friends," she said, "they are speaking German! Of course, I know some German but I am not able to understand exactly what they are saying."

"In other words, we may be in hostile territory," Barnaby fretted. "I must redouble my efforts to check these fuel gauges. Beauregard, see if you can help me figure out where we're losing power."

"Are we going to make it to D-Day?" Bridget inquired. "I'm getting sort of nervous with those guys outside. What if we're in Nazi Germany?"

"Stay cool," Babette smiled, borrowing one of Bridget's lines. "We'll be on our way as soon as Barnaby and Beauregard figure out the problem. Let's take a peek at our German friends."

Bridget and Babette peered out through the port hole one more time to see what was going down outside. The men had called in reinforcements. They were swarming over the airplane looking for clues.

"I'm getting more nervous by the second," Bridget declared. "How much time do we have before the cloaking device needs a rest?"

"I really have no idea," Babette said, as she continued to look out of the port hole. "Maybe we should remind Barnaby of the time limitation."

"You might be right," Bridget replied. "Hey, guys! What's our time limit?" she yelled.

As Babette watched, all the Germans looked toward the cloaked time machine. They had heard Bridget's voice! The cloaking device was beginning to fail! Babette hurried down the ladder.

"The cloaking device...it's not working...they can hear us!" she cried. "Do something, before they damage the time machine!"

Suddenly, they could hear tapping and knocking on the surface of the ship. In the nick of time, Barnaby and Beauregard emerged triumphantly from the small engine room at the back of *Lady Liberty*.

"We found the problem," Barnaby announced, who didn't seem to have heard the fuss going on outside. "One of my socks caused a short in the power generator. Now we'll start to store power again."

Babette gave a hopeless sort of moan.

"One of your socks!" yelled Bridget. "Get this thing moving, Barnaby! They're knocking on the hull of the time machine!"

Barnaby flew into motion, punching buttons, setting dials. The droning hum of the engines filled the cabin. The lights flickered. They were off!

"Whew! Please! No more pit stops, especially in German territory in the middle of World War II!" Bridget said, starting to relax. Then, a strange look crossed her face. "You know, if any of those guys were hanging on to the outside of the ship, they would still be there, right?"

"I guess we'll find out when we reach our next destination," Beauregard answered.

A certain amount of tension suddenly returned to the atmosphere. The drone of the engines ceased and quiet ruled the cabin. No one moved, listening instead for sounds on the ship's surface. Silence.

"We're safe, I think," Barnaby said. "Let's take a look outside to see where we are."

"Hold on a minute," Bridget reminded them. "We know very little about World War II. Maybe we should ask Dad to give us a little background before we hit D-Day."

"Excuse me," Beauregard interjected. "I think perhaps the computer can help us out here. We would be wise to take advantage of the moment. After all, we're already here."

"I think you're right, Beauregard," Barnaby said. "Let me see what information the computer can offer us."

A few minutes later, Barnaby produced a short narrative that gave the time travelers additional information. Here's what they read:

World War II

The United States did not enter World War II until December 7, 1941, when Japan led a surprise attack on Pearl Harbor, Hawaii. The attack was so effective that most of the American Pacific fleet was sunk or badly damaged. President Franklin D. Roosevelt called the attack a "day of infamy" that would never be forgotten. The United States declared war on the Axis Powers (Germany, Italy, and Japan) and began the long, difficult task of fighting a two-ocean war. In 1941, most of Europe was in the grip of Nazi Germany. In the Pacific, the Japanese continued to conquer the islands of the Pacific Rim, extending their domination over most of the South Pacific. There was little to stop their rapid expansion after the devastating attack on Pearl Harbor. However, the Axis Powers had grossly underestimated the industrial might of the United States. American industry went into wartime production, creating more ships, more armaments, and more aircraft than the fascist dictators could have anticipated.

Halting the tide of aggression unleashed by the dictatorships took a tremendous effort on the part of the United States and the Allies. At first, the Axis Powers held on to their conquered territory. Then, in 1942, the Allies opened a second front in North Africa, with General Dwight D. Eisenhower in command. American troops were unseasoned and this campaign gave them the experience they needed. With the defeat of the Axis Powers in North Africa, the Nazis could no longer dominate the Mediterranean Sea. The Allies invaded Sicily and attacked Italy. The most difficult task, however, was the Allied invasion of Normandy on June 6, 1944. With a successful landing in northern France, the Allies could strike a decisive blow to the heart of Nazi Germany. In this sense, D-Day was the beginning of the end for Hitler and the totalitarian domination of Europe. By the end of April, 1945, both Mussolini and Hitler were dead. On May 7, 1945, the Germans surrendered and the war in Europe was over.

The Pacific theater was another matter. When the Allies finally reconquered Europe, the invasion of Japan was yet to be undertaken. President Roosevelt died at the beginning of his fourth term in office in April 1945, leaving the decision up to his successor, Harry S. Truman. The United States had secretly been working on a new weapon that unleashed the power of the atom. The atomic bomb had never been used before but its creators knew it had immense destructive capability. Truman and his advisors decided to drop the atomic bomb on Japan to save lives on both sides and to bring an immediate end to the war in the Pacific. The United States dropped two atomic bombs, on Hiroshima and Nagasaki, which forced the Japanese to surrender on August 15, 1945. The massive destruction of these two bombs changed the face of history forever. Seventy-eight thousand people died in Hiroshima from one bomb. And many more people died in the months and years that followed. Unborn generations suffered genetic damage from the atomic bomb's long-term effects.

A cold war quickly developed between the western democracies and the Soviet Union, where totalitarianism had taken hold in the form of communism in 1917, during World War I. The Union of Soviet Socialist Republics was led by Joseph Stalin throughout World War II. Stalin was a mass murderer—he killed millions of his own people because he believed they were not loyal followers of Stalinist communism. Although Stalin had been united with the Allies in resisting fascist aggression, the post-war period saw heightened tensions between them.

Throughout the fifties, sixties, and seventies, Americans learned that communism was the new enemy. The opposing sides in the so-called Cold War engaged in massive arms races, building huge nuclear stockpiles and long-range ballistic missiles capable of delivering nuclear bombs many times more powerful than those dropped on Japan. Weapons of mass destruction brought a new detachment from the horrors of war. A push of a button could destroy millions of people. However, the threat of nuclear destruction left an indelible imprint on the imaginations of the Americans who grew up with this threat of destruction.

By the time Bridget, Babette, Barnaby, and Beauregard had read the last sentence, they realized how fortunate they were to be living in an era where the threat of nuclear destruction was greatly diminished.

"I see we've picked an auspicious moment in history to visit," Beauregard said, breaking the silence. "Are you ready for a look at D-Day?

Bridget, Babette, and Barnaby scrambled to their feet, ready to check out the largest invasion force ever assembled. As they peeked through the port hole, they were surprised to see they had arrived at night. They were situated on a cliff above the English Channel. The low tide and full moon made it an ideal evening to launch an invasion.

"Will we be able to see anything from this position?" Bridget asked. Suddenly, they heard the sounds of aircraft overhead. "I guess we won't see anything until daybreak," she added. "But it sure sounds like we've arrived at the right moment."

"Should we set the timer or the cloaking device for the evening?" Barnaby asked his comrades. "I doubt that we are in any danger of detection at this height."

Just as he had finished speaking, two jeeps carrying British Army personnel pulled up next to *Lady Liberty*. They looked like they were in a hurry. They surrounded the time machine.

"Here we go again," Bridget moaned. "We'd better get outside before these guys think we're here to start trouble."

As soon as the group emerged from the hatch, they were confronted by the British commanding officer, who was obviously disturbed by their unauthorized presence in the vicinity of the coming invasion.

"Right! Would you mind telling me how you came to be located at this position? Are you aware that you and your...vehicle are in a restricted area?" the officer demanded. "I am Captain Julius T. Bluster of His Majesty's Special Forces.

"Bluster? Did you say your name was Captain Bluster?" Barnaby asked politely. "I have heard that name before!"

"Did any of your ancestors spend time in the United States prior to the Revolution?" Bridget asked. "Your face seems so familiar."

Obviously distracted from the task at hand, Captain Bluster beamed with delight. "Why yes, as a matter of fact, my great, great grandfather was Captain Horatio Hornblower Bluster. He was stationed in the colonies for a while during your Revolution," he said. "How did you come to know my family's name?"

"We have traveled extensively and completed some historical research," Babette said, sounding very intellectual. "You might say that we have had personal contact with your ancestor—in a manner of speaking, of course."

Everyone tittered.

"Splendid news!" Captain Bluster shouted, obviously elated. (He did seem to shout quite a bit, but then, it was a family characteristic.) "I gather you must be continuing your historical investigations here today," he said smiling.

"Precisely," Babette continued. "We wanted to see the invasion from a proper perspective."

The captain frowned. "Hmm. How do you know about the invasion? Your clothing is certainly unusual, although I rather like your "Yanks" cap, young lady," he said. "But I think I'll have to bring you in for questioning. Your presence is somewhat disturbing, to say the least."

The time travelers were loaded into the jeeps and whisked away to the army headquarters, which also happened to be the location for coordinating the D-Day invasion. Captain Bluster chatted amicably with the foursome, especially about his ancestors, and soon everyone was enjoying the company of the strange young people and the cat who had stumbled into the staging area for D-Day.

"Would you like to see the war room?" Captain Bluster asked unexpectedly. "But our visit must be very brief. Come dawn, we'll be throwing everything we've got at the Nazis."

As they entered the war room, the time travelers saw a huge map of the invasion, complete with ship and aircraft positions, spread out before them. Captain Bluster explained that the plan was to establish five landing beaches. Paratroopers were already dropping behind enemy lines to help prepare the way for the invasion. An armada of ships twenty miles wide was waiting to bring the Allied troops to the Normandy beaches, and nine thousand aircraft were ready to attack. It was a crucial moment in World War II, and a very exciting place to be.

Captain Bluster ushered them out of the war room and offered them refreshments, which they gladly accepted. It was the middle of the night and Captain Bluster would be a very busy man in just a few short hours. The time travelers were weary and ready for sleep.

"I must apologize for the lack of sleeping accommodations at this facility," the captain said. "I'm afraid I must return you to your vehicle quite shortly. At dawn you will see the invasion quite clearly from your vantage point."

"Thank you, Captain Bluster, for showing us around," Bridget said. "We will always remember your kindness."

As they parted company, the captain looked at them and said, "Thank you for the anecdotes about my family history. If you ever visit this time and place again, please bring me something that belonged to Captain Horatio Hornblower Bluster, if your paths cross again—in a manner of speaking, of course."

Everyone tittered.

When the group had settled in for the night, they chatted briefly about the day's events. Then Beauregard set the alarm clock so they wouldn't miss the invasion. They would have very little sleep that night.

"Can you believe that we met a relative of that British Army captain we encountered in Richmond?" Bridget said. "He sure wasn't the nicest guy I ever met."

"Well, back then, we were a British colony. Now, we're a British ally," Beauregard replied. "There's quite a big difference."

"Do you think he knew that we were—" Bridget didn't finish her question because Beauregard started to laugh.

"We will never know the answer to that question, Bridget!" he said. "He acted like he already knew us, in some respects. Maybe his great, great grandfather kept records of our visit."

The alarm clock rang all too soon, and the group was a little slow to get out of bed. Once they stepped outside, however, the spectacle before them was unforgettable. The roar of thousands of planes was deafening, and the vision of so many ships was overwhelming, but the thought of so many people facing death to win freedom from tyranny was truly ennobling. The time travelers stood in awe of the event.

Suddenly, a warning bell began to sound inside the time machine. Something was wrong! The group ran back inside to discover that a fuel cell indicator was running low. And this time, Barnaby's socks were nowhere to be found.

"We must head home for repairs immediately," Barnaby shouted. "Please prepare for an immediate return to the present!"

Before long, Dr. Tempus Fugit was asking them a zillion questions about their experiences. They were too tired to talk, but agreed to return in a few days to discuss their travels. When they got back to Bridget's home, they took long naps and woke just before dinner. They were full of questions now that they had recovered. They were also starving.

"Dad, do you remember life in the fifties?" Bridget asked. "We want to understand more about what happened during the Cold War.

"Wow! You guys have really been making time with those photo albums. Are you up to the old high school photographs already? Well, I can tell you, during the fifties, Eisenhower was elected president and the country returned to peaceful living," Bridget's dad replied. "Ike, as they called him back then, was worried about the threat of communism, but he was more worried about the impact of communism on military spending. He warned against the development of what he called the military industrial complex in America. As the Soviet Union grew more and more hostile to the United States, Eisenhower envisioned an arms race in which each country would try to become more powerful than the other. Joseph Stalin died in 1953 and the new Soviet leader, Nikita Khrushchev, was not less unfriendly. Eisenhower could see that the country would get into deeper and deeper debt by trying to keep up with the Russians. So, the Cold War was a delicate balance for him. After Eisenhower left office, the arms race began, just as he had predicted."

"Did this country enjoy a high degree of prosperity during those years?" Babette asked. "I know that the United States contributed huge sums of money to rebuild Europe after World War II. I believe it was called 'The Marshall Plan.'"

"Yes, the Eisenhower years were prosperous. There were plenty of jobs and people were spending money on all kinds of new appliances like television sets and dishwashers. Rock and roll had made its debut and Elvis Presley was the king. Young teenagers would hang out at the record store or soda shop and listen to the jukebox. They taught each other how to jitterbug and had big sock hops at their schools where they danced to music provided by the local disc jockey. Young women wore skirts, sweaters, bobby socks, and saddle shoes. Young men wore chinos and penny loafers, and some combed their hair into a style called a 'ducktail' like Elvis and other rock and roll stars. Hula hoops were big with the smaller kids. I think of the fifties as a prosperous, happy time to grow up. It was the beginning of the influence of the media in determining what clothes or cars we bought, what food we ate, even what new products we wanted. Television shows like *I Love Lucy* and *The Ed Sullivan Show* were immensely popular. And I always remember Walt Disney's *Wonderful World of Color*—it came on every Sunday evening. Gosh, you guys have really brought back some wonderful memories for me. I could talk about the fifties forever! I remember the time..."

"Wash those hands! Dinner is ready!" Bridget's mom called from the kitchen.

It almost felt like they were living in the fifties when they sat down as one big family at the dinner table. They ate a traditional meal of potatoes, meat, and vegetables, and finished up with cherry pie and ice cream.

"You know, I agree with your father about life in the fifties, but it wasn't the same for all Americans," Bridget's mom commented after dinner. "People of color had a life that was separate from those of white Americans. It wasn't until the sixties and seventies that the policy of segregation really began to be questioned. Before that, segregation kept people of color from enjoying their civil rights. People like Martin Luther King Jr. and Rosa Parks were responsible for beginning to change the social landscape for many minorities in the United States."

"You know, Mom, I really want to learn more about the sixties and seventies, too," Bridget replied. "I think I'll hit the sack early tonight and maybe we can talk more about those days tomorrow night."

As they headed off for a good night's rest, Barnaby said, "Let's visit the fifties tomorrow! I'd love to talk with some people our age about growing up in those times."

Bridget and Babette were quick to agree.

In the morning, the time travelers returned to the attic and found the old photograph albums still in the trunk where they had left them. They decided to take a quick look at some of them to see what they could recognize from the fifties. They were flipping through the pages when Babette noticed something unusual.

"When you flip these pages quickly," she said, "the people in the photos seem to move, almost like a movie. Here, let me show you."

Barnaby, Bridget, and Beauregard gathered around as Babette quickly flipped the pages of an old high school yearbook that she had discovered in the bottom of the trunk. The second time she did it, the time travelers found themselves sitting in a high school classroom with four or five students. The blackboard had a single word, "communism," written on it and the students were talking among themselves.

"Wha—what happened?" Bridget asked, rubbing her eyes. "Where are we?"

Babette, Barnaby, and Beauregard were equally stunned to find themselves in a discussion group, but then, they had learned to expect the unexpected when they investigated the treasures in Bridget's attic.

"We're having a small group discussion about communism," one of the students answered. "We're glad that you could join us."

"Well, now that I am here," Bridget said, "can somebody tell me what communism is? I'm really not sure that I know much about the subject."

The high school students looked at each other. They didn't seem to have a quick or easy definition to offer Bridget, but finally, one of them ventured an explanation.

"Well, communism was an economic system developed by Karl Marx, a philosopher who lived during the nineteenth century. Marx believed that most of the industrial nations had populations divided into two categories: 'haves' and 'have-nots.' The have-nots are the poor and Marx said that the trouble with capitalism is that the poor would only get poorer while the rich would only get richer. In order to avoid this, he proposed a society where everybody would own everything collectively, where everybody would be equal in every way. I guess you could think of it as some kind of ideal society, a utopia, and communism was supposed to evolve to the perfect state of existence. Of course, it didn't work that way." The young woman smiled politely. "Does that help?"

"Cool," Bridget said. "That helped quite a bit. So this guy Marx envisioned some kind of perfect society but it turned out to be another totalitarian dictatorship when it was attempted in the Soviet Union, correct?"

"As far as we know here in 1959," one of the students replied, "the Soviets are committed to destroying the western democracies. When somebody says they're going to bury you, I think you've got to take it as a serious threat, don't you?"

"Perhaps," Barnaby replied. "But maybe they meant that the communist system would prove to be superior in every way to the democratic system. So, in a sense, we would be buried by our failure to compete with them."

"That's an interesting assumption," another student responded. "But I haven't seen any evidence to support that argument. It looks like they want to bury us literally."

"If I understand you correctly," Babette said, "you are worried that the communists might attempt to conquer the world?"

Strange looks came across the faces of the fifties students. Finally, one of them asked. "Don't you realize that we might eventually have to fight the Russians to prevent such a take over? I mean, they are our major competitors and they do intend to spread their ideas by force, if necessary. The threat you mention is very real!"

Bridget, Babette, Barnaby, and Beauregard had no idea how they would get back to the attic, but they realized that these fifties kids had every reason to be worried about the future. There was no information that could contradict the arguments they were making, at least, not then. They decided to change the subject.

"So, what do you do for fun?" Bridget asked. "I mean, what do you with your spare time?"

The teenagers laughed and one of them said, "Come on, we'll show you!"

As the group left the classroom, the kids picked up the sounds of rock and roll in the distance. The closer they got to the high school gym, the louder the music got. When they got there, they took off their shoes like all the other students, who were dancing on the gym floor. The DJ was blasting a favorite, "Rock Around the Clock," by Bill Haley and His Comets.

"Wow! That looks like a cool dance!" Bridget said. "Sort of reminds me of the Charleston, somehow."

"The what?" one of the teenagers asked. "I don't think the jitterbug looks like the Charleston at all. Come on, I'll show you!"

Again, the time travelers learned quickly, and they were soon dancing the night away! Finally, during an intermission, Bridget noticed a high school yearbook sitting on the bench next to her. It looked exactly like her dad's version, only it was much newer. She called her friends together.

"Are you ready to go home?" she asked, showing them the yearbook. "We can always see if it will work again."

Babette, Barnaby, and Beauregard crowded around Bridget and stared intently at the photographs, hoping that they would spring to life again. Suddenly, they were sitting in Bridget's attic.

"Wow! What a dream," Bridget said. "I thought Dad's old yearbook had really come alive."

"It did, Bridget," Barnaby said. "It did."

✍ QUIZ #7 ✍
War and Peace: The Forties and Fifties

1. Who was the president of the United States during the First World War?

2. What was the name of the treaty that ended the First World War?

3. Who became Chancellor of Germany in 1933, beginning his reign of terror as a fascist dictator?

4. Who was president of the United States during the Depression and the Second World War from 1933 until 1945, when he died in office?

5. The United States entered the Second World War when Japan attacked what place?

6. Who was the Supreme Allied Commander at D-Day?

7. What is the name given to nineteenth-century philosopher Karl Marx's ideal state, in which everyone shares common ownership?

8. What countries made up the Axis powers in the Second World War?

9. Who made the decision to use atomic weapons to bring a quick end to the war in the Pacific?

10. Who was the ruthless dictator of the Soviet Union during the Second World War?

✍ Food for Thought ✍

Here are some questions that challenge you to find out more about the world wars and the cold-war era. If you don't see a question you like, make up your own! Record your responses in your journal, and remember that there may be more than one answer to these questions.

1. One of the major causes of the First World War was a system of "entangling alliances," the Triple Entente and the Triple Alliance. Could the First World War have been avoided if these alliances had been inoperative?

2. Franklin D. Roosevelt served the United States as president for an unprecedented four terms. In your estimation, why was Roosevelt so popular with the common people?

3. Harry Truman and his advisors made a very difficult decision to use the atomic bomb to end the war with Japan. Do you agree with the decision to use the bomb? Why or why not?

4. Watch television for an hour with the sound turned down. Pay close attention to the commercials. How many are there? How often do they occur? Are there any repeats? How do you think commercials influence television viewers?

5. When rock and roll made its appearance in the 1950s, many people thought that the music was not healthy for young people. Why? What are the roots of rock and roll?

✐ **Group Activities** ✑

Here are some activities that are suitable for several people. Choose one that interests you and your group and have fun completing it. Remember to set realistic goals and to define each member's role before you begin. Enjoy!

1. Create your own musical skit about the 1950s. Choose the music, the fashions, and the subject of the skit so that they accurately reflect the attitudes and beliefs you wish to portray. Stage the production for your families, friends, and classmates.

2. Create a rock music timeline. Illustrate the timeline with photographs and drawings of as many musicians as possible. Which musicians were most influential?

3. By 1960, 90 percent of American homes had a television. Watch several different fifties television shows such as *I Love Lucy*, *Gunsmoke*, and *The Ed Sullivan Show*. Choose your own shows, if you prefer. Create your own history of television based on the shows you have watched and any other information you can find.

4. During the world wars, women had to do the work that men had previously done. How did this influence people's attitudes about women? Create a skit that shows how the wars influenced the lives of women. Don't forget to include the lives of women in the military.

5. What role did the motion picture industry play in the Second World War? How did Hollywood stars use their fame to help the war effort? Who were these people and what did they do?

Chapter 9
Changes: The Sixties and Seventies

1954	*Brown v. Board of Education* decision reverses *Plessy v. Ferguson* (1896)
1955	Rosa Parks arrested and fined for breaking segregation laws; Reverend Dr. Martin Luther King, Jr. leads a successful bus boycott in Montgomery, Alabama
1960	John F. Kennedy elected president
1963	Civil rights march on Washington where Dr. King delivers the "I Have a Dream" speech; President Kennedy assassinated; Betty Friedan's *"The Feminine Mystique"* is published
1965	Caesar Chavez leads a successful grape boycott
1968	Reverend Dr. Martin Luther King and Robert F. Kennedy are assassinated; Stonewall ignites gay and lesbian civil rights movement
1969	First Moon landing
1972	United States withdraws from Vietnam
1973	President Nixon resigns following Watergate scandal; Supreme Court decides *Roe v. Wade* on abortion rights

"You know," Bridget confessed, "we've made it through some pretty tough moments together since we first started time traveling." Bridget, Barnaby, Babette, and Beauregard were seated at the breakfast table discussing what they wanted to see next. "I'm ready to tackle all the changes that took place in the sixties and seventies," Bridget continued, "civil rights, women's rights, Vietnam and the peace movement, migrant workers' rights, Watergate— you know, all the big ones. I'm just not sure where to start."

"Well, just remember that Dr. Tempus has warned us about our fuel reserves," Barnaby said. "I'd like to learn more about all of those things too, but we need to pack light and fly low, if you know what I mean."

"You Americans are so tricky with your images," Babette commented. "I gather that means you will be wearing the same pair of socks you wore at the sock hop on our next trip?"

Everybody laughed. "I think you've got the general idea, Frenchie," Bridget said. "Barnaby is also emphasizing the limits of the time machine. So how do we get to see all those things with depleted fuel reserves?"

"Well, if we visit certain places at the right moments, we could still see most of them," Beauregard said. "For instance, Washington, D.C. would be a great location to check out some of the protest movements."

"That sounds like a good idea," Bridget replied. "Why don't we visit Dr. Tempus this afternoon? We owe him a visit anyway and maybe he has some ideas."

Dr. Tempus Fugit had been anxiously awaiting their return visit. The time travelers told him about their narrow escapes with the cloaking device and about the fuel problem. He was quite concerned, especially about the fuel, and he agreed that they now needed to be very selective about their time traveling.

"Why don't we do a little research," Dr. Tempus suggested, "and see if we can pinpoint some appropriate moments to visit? If you set the timer and abide by its limitations, you shouldn't have any problem returning to the present."

"I've heard Mom and Dad comment about the civil rights movement but I don't know much about it," Bridget volunteered. "Maybe that would be a good place to start."

"The civil rights movement really started in the fifties, Bridget, in Montgomery and Birmingham, Alabama," Dr. Tempus Fugit began. "I think we could use Alabama and the South as a starting point and proceed from there."

"That sounds like a reasonable method to me," Barnaby replied. "But, speaking of your parents, Bridget, I'm wondering if they might also be helpful. I bet they know lots of the background information."

"You are right, Barnaby," Babette added. "Bridget's mom was talking about Dr. Martin Luther King Jr. and Rosa Parks just the other evening. We should talk to them some more about the civil rights movement."

That evening, Bridget's dad cooked dinner, while her mom sat down for a discussion with the group. Being a lawyer, she knew a lot about the civil rights movement. She started by giving them a brief history.

"Well, I'm sure you already know that segregation became the status quo in America after the Civil War. No sooner was slavery abolished than segregation was introduced. In 1896, the Supreme Court ruled that the races could be kept separate as long as the facilities provided were equal. That court case, *Plessy* v. *Ferguson*, made segregation legal. So, schools, movie theaters, lunch counters, buses, bathrooms, and water fountains, were separated by race. Separate schools were built for black and white children, but the amount school boards spent on the schools was seldom equal.

"In 1954, the Supreme Court reversed the *Plessy* decision and established integration as the law of the land in *Brown* v. *Board of Education*. Unfortunately, it wasn't that simple. Twenty-one states still had segregated schools and people's attitudes weren't going to change overnight. African Americans began to stage protest marches and rallies to win their rights. Of course, many of these protests began in the South before the *Brown* decision became the law of the land. Rosa Parks, for example, lived in Montgomery, Alabama where segregation was actively practiced.

"Black Americans were expected to move to the rear of the bus and to give up their seats to a white person if the bus was full. In December 1955, Rosa Parks was seated in the black section of the bus when the bus driver demanded that she give up her seat for a white man. Rosa Parks refused, and was sent to jail. The entire African American community was outraged that she suffered such an indignity. They asked the Reverend Dr. Martin Luther King to lead a boycott of Montgomery's buses. King was a young minister, only twenty-six years old, and he had recently moved to Montgomery. He accepted.

"As it turned out, Rosa Parks was tried and found guilty of violating Montgomery's laws and was fined $14. But that was before the bus boycott got under way. I suppose you could say her arrest acted as a catalyst for the boycott.

Dr. King did not believe in violence. In fact, he believed in nonviolent protest as a means to achieve social change. Marches, demonstrations, sit-ins, boycotts…they're all ways you can stand up for what you believe in without harming other people, and under King's leadership that is what the African American community did in order to protest against segregation. What happened? When the *Brown* decision was handed down several months later, it ended the need for the boycott by outlawing segregation.

"Well, the South decided to take its time about integration; some schools even had to be integrated with the help of federal troops. It's hard to understand how that might happen, but it did. African American children were escorted to school by federal troops armed with machine guns to protect them from snipers and the Ku Klux

Klan. In 1963, Dr. King traveled to Birmingham because everything was still segregated in that city. He organized marches and demonstrations, and was jailed. The police used violent methods to break up the demonstrations, including attack dogs and fire hoses. Nevertheless, the fight for freedom went on.

"In August 1963, a civil rights march took place in Washington, D.C. on the steps of the Lincoln Memorial with at least 250,000 people in attendance. That's where Dr. King delivered his famous "I Have a Dream" speech, which still stirs the hearts and minds of people today. All those people had assembled because they wanted federal legislation to guarantee their civil rights. The year 1963 was the one-hundredth anniversary of the Emancipation Proclamation.

"President Kennedy had sent civil rights legislation to Congress and the march helped to draw worldwide attention to the injustices that made federal legislation necessary. Two years later Selma, Alabama was still totally segregated. A march was organized from Selma to Montgomery but it was met with tear gas and billy clubs from the state police. Dr. King organized a ministers' march from Selma to Montgomery six days later and, with the help of the National Guard, completed the march in five days. By the time they reached Montgomery, 25,000 people had joined the march. It was the beginning of a long, difficult battle that echoes throughout the last thirty years of American history."

The time travelers had been listening with rapt attention. Bridget's mom sat quietly for a moment, reflecting on the struggle for justice. The freedom to go where you want to go, to do what you want to do, to be who you want to be, is the birthright of every American.

"Mom, do you think that the civil rights movement influenced Americans to use social protest as a way of expressing their desire for equal rights? I mean, the Vietnam War protests, the women's rights movement…were they influenced by Dr. King's nonviolent protest approach?"

"Well, in some ways, I think so," Bridget's mom responded. "You see, the country was ready for change, and almost all these struggles could be seen almost every night on television. Many Americans were shocked at what they saw, and it influenced what they thought. Americans have the right to petition the government to change its policies, and civil rights movements exercised that right."

"Well, I know that's not the whole story," Bridget said, "but it's a very good beginning. I'd still like to find out how the civil rights movement affected other groups."

"I think that would be interesting, too," Barnaby commented. "I remember hearing about a grape boycott by the migrant farm workers during that time."

"Well, that's another story," Bridget's dad said, coming into the family room. "And so is the women's movement and the Native American movement."

"It seems as though the entire United States was seeking justice during those years," Babette observed. "They must have been very difficult times."

"Change is never easy," Beauregard said. "Just think of the times you've attempted to change a habit that you know is bad for you. It might take a long time, but if you work at it, you can do it."

"Well, that's what it was all about during the sixties and seventies," Bridget's dad replied." The civil rights movement empowered many different minorities to seek their lawful rights."

"How about that grape boycott Barnaby was talking about?" Bridget asked. "Why did that happen?"

"Well, a man called Cesar Chavez organized Hispanic farm workers in California into a union so that they could earn better wages and demand safer working conditions," Bridget's dad responded. "Chavez considered the workers' long hours, poor wages, and terrible working conditions to be inhumane. He learned about nonviolent protesting from Dr. King, and organized the farm workers to go from farm to farm to spread the message, starting in 1962. By 1965, the farm workers had begun to boycott the grape farms, and new workers joined them. As a result, the fruit rotted on the vines. Chavez organized a 300-mile march across California to draw attention to the farm workers' cause, then he fasted for twenty-five days until farmers signed contracts with the union. It led to better pay and working conditions for Hispanic people who had been living in dire poverty for decades."

"What about Native Americans? They have suffered all kinds of injustices since the country was first founded," Bridget inquired. "I remember the Trail of Tears and the terrible mistreatment they received from the government. Did they start their own movement, too?"

"Yes, they did, Bridget," her dad responded. "Native Americans also learned the ways of nonviolent protest. They presented lists of grievances to the Bureau of Indian Affairs, but the government simply ignored them. So, they seized control of an old federal prison called Alcatraz, located on an island in San Francisco Bay. They held the prison for one and a half years. Next, they went to the Bureau of Indian Affairs in Washington, D.C. to stage a protest, and finally to Wounded Knee, South Dakota, where they occupied a trading post. Wounded Knee was where Native Americans had been slaughtered in 1890. The media attention they received through all these efforts did much to dramatize their plight. Native Americans began to receive better treatment from the courts, especially when they won arguments over rights established by treaties that the government had never honored."

"And what about the women's movement?" Babette asked. "Women began to demand equal pay for equal work, yes?"

Bridget's mom understood this struggle from first-hand experience. She responded to Babette's question with the knowledge and passion of a person who has learned through personal encounters with injustice.

"The women's movement for civil rights really began in the early 1960s, when a book entitled *The Feminine Mystique* by Betty Friedan was published. Friedan's book ignited a debate about the lives of women and the subservient roles they were expected to play. There was little opportunity for women to pursue careers as professionals—they were expected to sacrifice their ambitions for traditional homemaking and parenting roles. Yet, throughout the world war era, women had always done the work of men, usually for less pay. When women became active in the civil rights movement, they also learned how to protest the unequal treatment they were receiving. But not everyone agreed with the women's liberation movement. Some people felt that women should maintain the traditional roles. For example, when the Supreme Court decided that women have the right to choose an abortion in *Roe* v. *Wade* in 1973, the women's movement was strongly criticized by people who held traditional religious ideas. The debate about a woman's right to choose continues to this day.

"But the women's movement drew a lot of attention to the second-class status of women, and professional opportunities for educated women began to improve. More women were admitted to law and medical schools, and more women appeared in the business world. As a result of the women's movement, women began to develop more opportunities for themselves and for their daughters. Now girls in elementary school could talk about their ambitions to be doctors and lawyers or to join the fire brigade or police force. The key, however, is still education. For many poor women of all races, things have not improved. Without an education, it is hard for anyone, regardless of sex or race, to improve their chances in life."

"And don't forget that gay people have fought for their civil rights, too," Bridget's dad interjected. "Ever since the famous Stonewall riots here in New York City in 1968, gay and lesbian activists have worked to overcome discrimination in the work place, in the military, and in marriage laws. Their struggle is still visible today, especially as they deal with people who hold highly traditional religious values. Just like abortion rights, gay rights issues upset people who believe that alternative lifestyles violate traditional moral values."

"I never realized that so many groups had to work so hard for justice in America," Barnaby said. "I've always associated the sixties and seventies with excessive drug experimentation and loud rock music. I think I need to look at this era with a new perspective, since it seems it was also a very turbulent, violent time."

"Well, three very good leaders lost their lives to the assassin's bullet in the sixties," Bridget's dad replied. "I'll never forget that day in November 1963 when President John F. Kennedy was assassinated by Lee Harvey Oswald in Dallas, Texas. The whole nation was so traumatized by the event that the memory can still bring tears to people's eyes. Then, five years later, the Reverend Dr. Martin Luther King and Robert Kennedy were assassinated within three months of each other. It's hard to imagine that three people who were so well loved could also be hated that intensely."

"You know, the problem with memories is that they sometimes stir up all the emotions you felt when something actually happened," Bridget's mom continued. "I guess that's why people should study history—so they will remember and relive past events. There's so much to reflect upon, so many choices to make. Without history, how would we ever know who we really are or where we really want to go in life?"

"What else do you remember about those days, Mom and Dad?" Bridget asked abruptly. "I want to know more."

"You aren't tired of all these stories?" Bridget's dad laughed. "I thought you might be worn out by now!"

"I have always wondered about the Vietnam era," Babette interjected. "I know that the war had a profound effect on American culture."

"Well, the war in Vietnam was a very painful experience for Americans," Bridget's dad began. "Four American presidents, Eisenhower, Kennedy, Johnson, and Nixon all had to deal with the problems of a war that was fought to contain the spread of communism in Southeast Asia. It happened because we got involved in a civil war between North and South Vietnam. The American people supported the presidents, who gradually increased our involvement in the war to stop communism from spreading to South Vietnam. But North Vietnam's leader, Ho Chi Minh, was determined to unify his country. To the Vietnamese, he was a patriot. To Americans, he was another potential communist dictator.

"The United States envisioned a unified communist threat from the Soviet Union, China, and Vietnam. Little did we know when we got involved that the Chinese and the Vietnamese really didn't get along so well! We spent billions of dollars dropping tons of bombs and napalm on the jungles of that very poor country trying to defeat the communists. But they knew the jungles and the countryside much better than we did. Finally, in 1972, the United States withdrew from Vietnam, leaving the country to determine its own destiny. It was a very costly mistake in terms of lives lost and money spent. It also left some terrible images in the minds of Americans, images of massacred civilians and saturation bombing. President Lyndon B. Johnson's entire 'war on poverty' was ultimately undermined by the excessive military spending on the Vietnam War. In the end, he was so demoralized by the increasingly strong protest movement that he decided not to run for re-election in 1968.

"When the Democratic National Convention met in Chicago in 1968, the anti-war movement was there. Violence broke out in the streets, with policemen clubbing the protesters while they chanted, 'The whole world is watching!' Richard Nixon was elected president in 1968 and again in 1972. It was Nixon who finally withdrew the United States from Vietnam, but not until after another five years of bloodshed and wasting billions of dollars more."

"Whenever I think of President Nixon, I think of his resignation from office," Barnaby said. "Wasn't he almost impeached because of the Watergate scandal?"

"That's a great question, Barnaby," Bridget's mom said. "Nixon was a very paranoid man. He kept enemies' lists, wiretapped phones, and ordered his people to bug Democratic headquarters in a classy building in Washington, D.C. called the Watergate Hotel. He wanted to know more about the strategies that the Democrats planned to use against him during his re-election bid in 1972. He also wanted to find out private information about the lives of his opponents. Nixon's advisors hired burglars to break into Democratic headquarters and steal documents. Then, when people began to investigate these crimes, the White House advisors offered to pay them to keep quiet. Two reporters from the *Washington Post*, Bob Woodward and Carl Bernstein, exposed the whole scandal in the newspapers. Congressional investigations into the matter continued until there was enough evidence to begin impeachment proceedings against President Nixon. He resigned before he could be removed from office.

"Nixon's vice president, Spiro Agnew, had resigned earlier because of tax fraud, leaving the presidency to the newly selected vice president, Gerald Ford. President Ford pardoned Nixon, believing that the country could no longer stand the misery of a trial. It really was a national disgrace and a terrible blight on the office of the president. One good thing, however, was that the Constitution worked. The president of the United States was caught breaking the law, and he was forced to resign for his wrongdoing."

"Let me ask you one thing," Bridget said. "How do you remember all of this stuff? I mean, it's amazing how much you know about this era."

"If you had lived through some of those times, you wouldn't forget them either, Bridget," her dad responded. "And your mother and I have been interested in history for a long time! Why do you think we've got all those treasures in the attic?"

"Now I think I understand the sixties and seventies a little better, thanks to your memories," Bridget replied. "I'll have to tell my kids these stories one day, when they're old enough to appreciate them, of course."

Bridget's parents laughed out loud at her comments, but they were also very pleased that Bridget, Babette, Barnaby, and Beauregard wanted to know more about the past. It was part of their lives, part of themselves that they were eager to share. The night had grown late, however, later than anyone had anticipated. After all, time flies when you're having fun!

The next morning, the group decided where they wanted to go next. It was time to travel once again! They agreed to pinpoint several places to visit in order to conserve fuel.

"I still think that Washington, D.C. is the place to be," Beauregard reminded them. "So many events occurred in the nation's capital during that time."

"Well, I know I want to hear Dr. King's 'I Have a Dream' speech, and that occurred in 1963 during the civil rights march," Bridget announced. "Why don't we start there?"

Dr. Tempus Fugit was in quite an excited state. *Lady Liberty* was ready to roll, but he was still trying to figure out the fuel cell depletion.

"Could Barnaby's sock have created a permanent biochemical imbalance in the cell?" he wondered to himself. "I'll have to replace the entire cell, if that's the case. But I really won't know until they return from their next time voyage!"

"Ah, here you are, Dr. Tempus," Babette said, as they congregated in his office. "We would like to travel to the sixties and seventies today. Is the ship ready for us?"

"Yes, but I must caution you again to remember the limits of the timing and cloaking devices. I guess I still have a few bugs to work out!" Dr. Tempus replied.

"Bugs? Dr. Tempus, there are no insects on board!" Babette protested.

"No, no, Babette. I mean problems to work out, not insects," Dr. Tempus chuckled. "I think you'd better prepare yourselves for immediate departure."

Lady Liberty's engines droned to life with the usual hum and flickering lights that her occupants had grown to enjoy. Somehow, those sounds provided reassurance and comfort, a home-away-from-home kind of feeling. The tempometer was set for 1963.

When they arrived, the time travelers opened the hatch to the sound of thousands of people. They had landed behind a grove of trees right next to the civil rights march! They climbed out of the ship and made their way over to the crowd. Then, they sat down to listen and to learn about the civil rights movement from the speakers and from the people all around them.

People shared food, sang songs and, most importantly, they shared their hopes for a brighter future. Late in the afternoon, the last speaker stepped onto the podium. It was the Reverend Dr. Martin Luther King Jr. At first he spoke quite formally then, suddenly, he was speaking with the passion and conviction of a person who has known the trials and tribulations of injustice:

> I have a dream that one day in Alabama…little black boys and black girls will be able to join hands with little white boys and white girls as sisters and brothers…
>
> I have a dream today! I have a dream that my four little children will one day live in a nation where they will not be judged by the color of their skin, but by the content of their character. I have a dream today!

The time travelers were soon caught up with Dr. King's inspirational speech; they felt the hopes that all the people at that march felt on that hot August day. They heard the words of the famous song, "We Shall Overcome," which had become the anthem of the civil rights movement. They held hands and sang the words along with all the people around them.

> *We shall overcome,*
> *We shall overcome,*
> *We shall overcome, someday.*
> *Oh, deep in my heart,*
> *I do believe,*
> *We shall overcome someday.*

By the time the peaceful rally ended, the time travelers knew that they had witnessed something wonderful. They talked about it as they walked back to the time machine.

"I'll never forget Dr. King's voice," Bridget said. "He was really quite a gifted leader."

"He was wonderful," Babette agreed. "But so were all the people who came to demonstrate. It was a huge crowd, yet so peaceful."

As they reached the time machine, Barnaby and Beauregard did a quick check and found everything in good working order. It was time to choose their next destination.

"I want to talk to some of the people who protested the Vietnam War," Barnaby said. "Let's set the tempometer for 1968 and see where we land."

It was a short, well-placed hop. A pro-Vietnam War rally was going on at that very moment in the city square. Banners saying things like "Support Our Boys in Vietnam!" were everywhere. It was a candlelight vigil, and many people had turned out to demonstrate their support for the war effort.

Bridget, Barnaby, Babette, and Beauregard joined the crowd. Suddenly, somebody yelled, "There they are, over there, those cowards!" The smell of hate filled the air. The crowd surged toward a small group of protesters who stood on the edge of the square. They also held posters and signs, but theirs said things like, "Support Our Boys in Vietnam, Bring Them Home Now!" The crowd shouted all kinds of ugly names, then began to throw eggs at the anti-war group. They literally chased them off the city square.

The time travelers followed the protesters and caught up with them several blocks away. They were mostly students from the nearby college, and a few of their professors. In total, there were about twenty people.

"What made you show up at a rally like that?" Bridget asked one of the students as she walked along beside him. "Didn't you know that those people were in favor of the war?"

"We believe that the war in Vietnam is immoral," the student answered. "People say that we must stop the spread of communism, but we don't believe that you can kill an idea with a gun. We feel we have a moral responsibility to protest; we want people to know that not everyone agrees with America's policies in Vietnam."

"I admire the courage of your convictions," Barnaby replied. "But wouldn't some people think that you are being a little naive? I mean, can you really stop a war by protesting?"

"We think so!" several of the students answered simultaneously.

As they continued along the city streets, they came across a construction site at the college where a wooden fence had been erected to keep people out of the area. It had been covered with paintings and slogans like "Peace Now!" But one of the slogans stood out from all the rest. It said, "War is not healthy for children and other living things," and was accompanied by a picture of a hand holding a colorful bunch of flowers. It was really very striking. The foursome parted company with the students, and turned to go back to *Lady Liberty*.

"Wow!" Bridget said. "I had no idea that this war protest thing was so intense! You know, I thought those college kids were going to get killed."

"I know what you mean," Barnaby replied. "At first, I wondered why people would put their lives in jeopardy just to show their disapproval. I understand their thinking better now. It was a matter of conscience for them. You can really start to see the influence of the civil rights movement from the way they explained themselves."

"You are right, Barnaby," Babette replied. "They felt that the Vietnam War was an injustice that they needed to protest. I was impressed with their arguments."

When they got back to *Lady Liberty*, Barnaby headed into the engine room again to assess the condition of the ship. It still appeared to be in excellent shape; they could head off somewhere else. This time, they chose 1972, the year that Richard Nixon's problems with Watergate began to surface.

The time travelers returned to Washington, D.C. intending to meet the man at the center of the scandal. They had no idea how that could be accomplished, but they were going to try. The cloaking device seemed like a good idea—after all, burglary was in vogue!

The three kids and the cat decided to go for a tour of the White House. They waited patiently in line and hoped to catch a glimpse of the president. They were in luck! Just as the tour came up to the president's office, Mr. Nixon emerged. He began shaking hands and chatting with the entire tour group.

The time travelers, knowing what was up, were not as gracious as some of the other visitors. Bridget was burning. Beauregard was standing next to his young friend, and Richard Nixon shook his paw. The president felt a prickly sensation. He then turned to Bridget and extended his hand.

"I want to know why you did it!" Bridget demanded. "Why did you break the law?"

Nixon blanched. "Well, er...er...I have no idea what you're talking about," he said gruffly and stormed off. When he got a short distance from the group, he turned around and shook a finger at them and said, "I'll tell you one thing! I am not a crook!"

"Sure," Bridget said under her breath. Beauregard bristled at her side. Babette and Barnaby tittered nervously, and tried not to look at the other members of the group.

When they finished the tour, Barnaby, Babette, Bridget, and Beauregard returned to *Lady Liberty* to find that the cloaking device had again drained the fuel. It was time to go home.

The drone of the engines sounded a little weaker this time, but there didn't appear to be any real problem. Then, suddenly, the ship began to shudder and shake. They looked at each other with wild expressions. They were already in flight!

"What's wrong, Barnaby?" Bridget yelled over the noise. "Are we going to make it?"

"I don't know," Barnaby yelled back. "I think somebody has sabotaged the time machine!"

✍ QUIZ #8 ◻

Changes: The Sixties and Seventies

1. Who refused to give up her seat on the bus in Montgomery, Alabama in 1955?

2. Who was the leader of the civil rights movement who was assassinated in 1968?

3. Who was the Hispanic leader of the grape boycott who won better pay and working conditions for the farm workers of California?

4. Who wrote *The Feminine Mystique*, the book which sparked the beginning of the women's movement?

5. What was the name of the trading post seized by Native Americans, which later became the site of a massacre?

6. The gay liberation movement began when protesters demonstrated at what place in New York City?

7. Which president resigned from office when he was caught breaking the law?

8. Which North Vietnamese leader was considered a patriot by his people?

9. What was the name of the Supreme Court decision that established a women's right to choose an abortion?

10. What Supreme Court decision reversed the "separate but equal" principle established by the *Plessy v. Ferguson* decision?

✍ Food for Thought ◻

These questions challenge you to express your own position about some of the issues that people faced during the 1960s and 1970s. Choose the questions that most interest you, and write your responses in your journal. Enjoy!

1. The struggle for civil rights, the struggle for freedom, took many forms during the 1960s and 1970s.

Take one of the groups mentioned in this book and write an "update" of its progress toward civil rights.

2. How did America's fear of communism influence this country's involvement in Vietnam? Why did it take so long for the United States to get out of Vietnam? Would you have volunteered to fight in Vietnam? Would you have gone to Vietnam if you had been drafted into the military?

3. If you had lived during the 1960s and 1970s, would you have supported any of the civil rights movements? Which one(s) would you have supported? Why? Which movement(s) do you support today?

4. In the America of the nineties, many people have resorted to violence and terrorism to achieve their goals. Why do you think groups resort to terror and gang violence to achieve their aims? What do you think of this?

5. Investigate the details of the Watergate scandal. Do you think that President Nixon's resignation was justified?

✍ Group Activities ✍

Here are some activities that you can do with other people who have similar interests! They give you the opportunity to use your knowledge in fun ways. Choose an activity that you and your group agree would be enjoyable. Be sure to set goals and assign roles for each group member. Enjoy yourselves!

1. Create a mural from a series of drawings or posters that depicts the struggle for civil rights. Include as many of the different movements as you want. Give the completed work a title that captures the main idea of your efforts.

2. Write a magazine article about your life as a young person during the seventies. What were the big

issues for young people? Assign each person in your group an issue. When everyone is finished writing, put the individual pieces together to form one article. Decide what the title of the article should be. Give it to some people who lived during those times and ask them what they think.

3. The 1960s and 1970s produced some excellent rock and folk artists: The Beatles; The Rolling Stones; Bob Dylan; Peter, Paul, and Mary; the Doors; Janis Joplin; Jimi Hendrix; Led Zeppelin; Eric Clapton; The Grateful Dead; Joan Baez; Joni Mitchell; Judy Collins; The Who; Jefferson Airplane/Starship; Crosby, Stills, Nash, and Young; Simon and Garfunkle; Frank Zappa and the Mothers of Invention, to name a few.

It was also the beginning of the Motown sound and soul music with excellent artists like: Martha and the Vandellas; Smoky Robinson and the Miracles; The Temptations; The Four Tops; Marvin Gaye; Diana Ross and the Supremes; Stevie Wonder; Aretha Franklin; Gladys Knight and the Pips, and the Jackson Five.

   a. Create a rock/folk hall of fame with photos, drawings, and posters of all the greats during the sixties and seventies. Place all the artists on a timeline.

   b. Using the Motown/soul sound, create a hall of fame with posters, drawings, and posters. Place the artists on a timeline.

   c. Now, using the timelines and doing your own research, identify the chief musical influences on rock music, on folk music, and on soul music.

   d. How does the music reflect the era of the sixties and seventies?

   e. Choose the artists that interest you most and trace their origins and the influences on their music.

Chapter 10
The Opulent Eighties

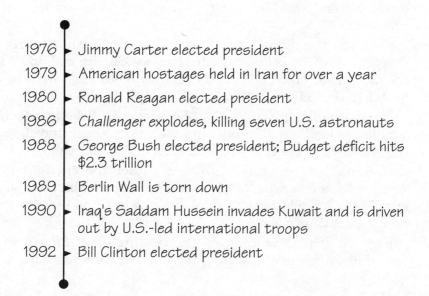

1976 ▸ Jimmy Carter elected president

1979 ▸ American hostages held in Iran for over a year

1980 ▸ Ronald Reagan elected president

1986 ▸ Challenger explodes, killing seven U.S. astronauts

1988 ▸ George Bush elected president; Budget deficit hits
       $2.3 trillion

1989 ▸ Berlin Wall is torn down

1990 ▸ Iraq's Saddam Hussein invades Kuwait and is driven
       out by U.S.-led international troops

1992 ▸ Bill Clinton elected president

Can you believe how fast time flies? Well, believe me, just lately it's been a fairly difficult ride—the turbulence of the world wars followed up by the social unrest of the sixties and seventies. Yet, I must say I've enjoyed every single moment of the adventures I've had with my human friends. Of course, I've had to curtail my carousing with the catnip crew but then, there were some very important people to meet, and some important things to do. I wonder if we'll ever get around to tackling world history. Now that would be a challenge!

Right now, I'm hoping that we can figure out what's causing this tailspin we're experiencing. Barnaby thinks the ship may have been sabotaged, but who would be capable of doing such a thing? Spies? Space aliens? I'll have to examine the situation closely to see if it's a serious problem. After all, I want to get back to Bridget's house in time for dinner!

✎ ✎ ✎ ✎ ✎

"Stop this thing, Barnaby!" Bridget yelled as they continued to thump and shudder along. "We've got to take a look at the problem!"

"You said you didn't want to make any more pit stops for repairs, Bridget," Barnaby yelled back, his hair shaking up and down with the movement of the ship. "How do you know that we'll be able to get it started again?"

"I have confidence in you and Beauregard," Babette yelled, her sunglasses jiggling. "I'm not sure we can continue traveling like this without causing permanent damage to the ship."

"I think I must agree with you, under the circumstances," Beauregard announced, his size actually keeping him quite steady, apart from his whiskers. "I think we'd better find out the source of the problem."

Barnaby began procedures for landing *Lady Liberty* safely. Sounding much like a rattling tin can, the time machine finally came to a grinding halt.

"Well, here we are, wherever that is," Barnaby sighed. "I guess we'd better check out our surroundings before we venture outside. I sure hope we're not walking into trouble."

"It would not be the first time!" Babette laughed, pushing her sunglasses back up from the end of her nose. "It is time for us to take a quick look around. Perhaps we have not gone anywhere?"

The time travelers crowded around the port hole for a look at their latest pit stop. They could see the Washington Monument, the Lincoln Memorial...they were still in the nation's capital, Washington, D.C.

"See?" Babette said. "I told you so! We just do not have enough power to get home, so we will have to figure out a way to boost our fuel reserves."

"So I guess we're still in 1972, right?" Bridget asked. "Well, we might as well make the best of it. And once we figure out what's wrong, we can be on our way."

Barnaby and Beauregard headed into the engine room to check out something Barnaby was calling a fuel cell depletion problem. Bridget and Babette decided to assist them.

"Babette and I will go outside and see if we notice anything unusual. If you need us, open the hatch and yell," Bridget said.

As soon as Bridget and Babette emerged from the hatch of *Lady Liberty*, they realized that at least one thing was quite different: It was very cold.

"It must be winter," Bridget said, shivering. "It's freezing out here! And look over there! There's all kinds of scaffolding and stuff. Looks like somebody's having a big party. Let's go tell Barnaby and Beauregard."

They climbed back down the hatch and headed into the engine room to inform their comrades of their discovery.

"It doesn't look like the same city to me," Bridget told Barnaby and Beauregard. "It's very cold and people are partying. We ought to check it out!"

"Well, we think we've found the problem," Barnaby announced. "One of the diamond laser connections has broken. That's the good news. The bad news is…we need another diamond to replace the one we've lost!"

"Where are we going to get a diamond?" Bridget wondered aloud. "I mean, we don't have a lot of money. Say, maybe we can find one!"

"Find one?" Babette asked. "How are we ever going to find a diamond? It would be easier to find out what year we are in, since it might be home for a while."

"Oh, don't be so pessimistic, Babette!" Bridget cajoled. "I think we ought to head toward those big parties we saw. I'll bet we can find a few diamonds there."

"Well, at least we know what we need," Barnaby replied. "It certainly wouldn't hurt to take a look around."

The time travelers bundled up in the old clothing Dr. Tempus had stored away for emergency use. They looked a little ragged, but at least they were warm when they stepped out into the cold winter's night.

As the time travelers walked down Fourteenth Street, they saw lots of homeless people sleeping in the doorways. Some of them were lying on top of large exhaust ducts that blew up a steady stream of warm air. Others were huddled in large cardboard boxes, or under a multitude of small ones, trying to keep warm.

"Those poor guys sure look cold," Bridget observed. "I wish I could help them out. You know, I don't think I've ever seen so many homeless people. What year could this be?"

Suddenly, they heard a deep voice behind them. "You don't know what year this is? You must be joking!"

The voice belonged to a man wearing what must have been expensive clothes. By now, however, they were beginning to look a little shabby.

Babette immediately dropped into karate attack position. She wasn't taking any chances. Beauregard quietly slipped off into the darkness, ready to pounce if the need arose. The kids stood there for just a moment while someone thought of something to say.

"Well, I'm not joking, Sir," Bridget began. "We've lost track of time, so to speak. We've been doing a lot of traveling lately. You know how it is when you lose track of time."

"Yeah, I know what you mean," the man replied. "You lose track of time when you're living on the streets, too. I lost my job a few weeks ago and I'm not sure if I can pay my bills anymore. Tell you what, I'll help you out if you help me out."

"Well, Sir, we don't really have any money," Barnaby responded. "But we'd be happy to help you out in any other way if we can."

"Come on, sit down here on this park bench with me and tell me what you want to know," he said. "Where do you want me to start?"

"Well, er, um...What year is this? Who is president? Why are there so many homeless on the streets? Know someplace we can find a diamond?" Bridget asked, like she was never going to talk again.

"Whoa, there, not so fast!" the man laughed. "Let me see... I'll start by telling you that you have arrived in the Reagan years, and this guy has been tough on the poor and good to the rich. He said he was going to cut government spending and reduce the deficit. Well, he did the exact opposite. He cut all the programs that provided money to the city's poor. He cut spending on environmental protection, education, and welfare. He increased defense spending and gave big tax breaks to businesses and the rich. The rich got richer and the poor got a lot poorer. And some of these folks that you see out here on the street belong in hospitals for the mentally ill. They had to release them because they didn't have enough money to house them any more. If they weren't considered violent, then out they went. It's a really big mess."

"Excuse me," Babette said, still somewhat on guard. "But I hear you say that Reagan 'cut spending' and this 'deficit' issue keeps coming up. Can you explain these things to me?"

"Now I *know* you guys are from another planet!" the man chuckled. "Everybody has been talking about cutting the size of the federal government since Jimmy Carter was president. Ronald Reagan made cutting the size of government a major campaign theme, and the way you cut government is to cut programs and spending. Let me put it this way, if you want to know what a government values most, look at the way it spends its money. For instance, Reagan threw all kinds of money into the defense budget to build the 'star wars' missile system which could block nuclear bombs from outer space! Anyway, communism finally collapsed because it just didn't work. The 'star wars' project turned out to be a huge, black hole in the budget. Here it is, 1988, and we've tripled the budget deficit to 2.3 trillion dollars! See what I mean? Reagan's budgets actually *increased* government spending. And when you spend huge sums of money, you end up borrowing from somewhere else to pay the interest on the loans. That's how the budget deficit grew to such enormous proportions. Don't forget, too, that the rich got big tax breaks, and so did businesses."

"Wait a minute," Bridget interrupted. "This sounds a whole lot like the twenties, when people used to party like there was no tomorrow! Coolidge was president and he believed that government should leave business alone. It was a prosperous time but people got deeper and deeper into debt and they had no way to pay it back. That's how the Great Depression started."

"I'm so impressed!" the man cried. "That analogy to Coolidge is a good one. Reagan admired Coolidge's approach to government. Coolidge and Reagan both believed in what's called 'trickle-down economics.' The money 'created' by giving tax breaks to businesses and the wealthy was supposed to be shared with the poor in the form of private donations to charities. And businesses were supposed to create new jobs and share their new wealth with their employees. It didn't happen. Greed became an acceptable human virtue. So, here we are with a huge national debt, and future generations are going to have to pay higher tax bills. Unemployment is on the rise again; the country is headed into a recession. It isn't a pretty picture."

"So what's the solution?" Bridget demanded. "What's the best way out of the situation?"

"If I knew the answer to that question," the man chuckled, "I'd be rich. I guess we're all going to have to learn how to live with higher tax bills and less government spending. Maybe we've got to figure out a way to balance the budget."

"I understand your problem with the Reagan presidency," Babette said, "but I don't understand why the American people elected him for two terms. Surely they knew Reagan was misleading them?"

"Well," the man began, "Reagan's personality was a big factor. He was a movie star and a television personality, whom people knew and liked. He knew how to talk to people and he was sincere in his beliefs. That's why they called him 'the great communicator.' He was good at using his television personality to convince people that he was right. He was also a real friend to the business community, and companies contributed large sums of money to help him get re-elected in 1984. He was a very popular president. Unfortunately, the whole country is going to have to pay a very high price for instituting some of his economic policies."

"It seems like one big nightmare," Barnaby said. "Do you think the next president will be any better?"

"That's an interesting question," the man said. "Reagan's vice president, George Bush, was elected to the presidency and all this scaffolding you see, the parties, are to prepare for his inauguration. Bush called 'trickle-down economics' by a different name several years ago when he campaigned against Reagan for the presidency—'voodoo economics.' I think he's a decent man. We'll just have to let history be the judge of his presidency. I mean, Carter was a decent man, but he just couldn't deal with the hostage crisis in an effective manner. Islamic fundamentalists in Iran held Americans hostage for four hundred and forty-four days and Carter couldn't get them out! It made him look very incompetent. Reagan won easily.

"But then Reagan also got lucky with the collapse of communism. That system had been crumbling for a long time but Reagan took the credit for its collapse with his get-tough-on-the-Russians policy. See, I've got this clipping from the newspaper. It's all about the failure of communism as an economic system. It looks as if the Russians couldn't pay for their defense spending either! That was where all their money was going too. Now, don't mistake me. There's nothing wrong with having a strong national defense. But I'm hoping we can cut some of this crazy military spending and get some of these poor folk off the street. We're not paying attention to the needs of ordinary citizens anymore."

"Thanks for the update," Bridget responded gratefully. "I guess our generation is going to inherit some big problems. Right now, actually, we've got a big problem. We've got to find a diamond to replace one that we've lost."

"But you've got one already!" the man laughed. "Look at your wristwatch. Doesn't it have a small diamond on its face?"

Bridget looked at her watch. The man was right! They could get home after all! They carefully removed the back of the watch with a small screwdriver that Barnaby produced from the inside of his lab coat. Then they removed the diamond and Barnaby put it in his pocket for the trip back to *Lady Liberty*.

"You've been so wonderful," Bridget said to the stranger. "I don't even know your name but I'd like to help you out. Here, take my watch. It's expensive! I saved my money for a long time to buy it, but I want you to have it."

"I can't accept your gracious offer," the man said politely. "I'll find a job soon. Things will get better, I know. I hope that you'll remember me when you get home and think about the ways your generation can make this a better country, a better world. One day, you'll be the decision makers, you'll be the problem solvers. I have faith in you."

When he had finished speaking, the man got up from the park bench and disappeared into the wintry night. It was a little eerie the way he vanished from sight so quickly but Bridget, Babette, Barnaby, and Beauregard would never forget him.

"Who was that guy?" Bridget asked, as they hustled back to the time machine. "I feel like I've met him before!"

"We'll never know," Barnaby said. "But he was a good human being."

When they reached the time machine, Barnaby rushed off into the engine room to repair the fuel cell connection with the diamond from Bridget's watch. It took only a couple of minutes. At last, they were ready to go home!

"We're ready for departure," Barnaby announced. "Prepare for launch!"

That primordial hum filled the cabin, the lights flickered dramatically, and *Lady Liberty* shot forth into the starry night. Within seconds, they arrived at the Statue of Liberty and went down into Dr. Tempus Fugit's laboratory. The first thing they saw was a huge table of food. The scientist was so looking forward to seeing them that he had prepared a special celebratory feast. He had also draped a huge, tie-dyed banner that said "Welcome Home" right across the laboratory.

"I've been so worried since you left," Dr. Tempus confessed. "I figured out the difficulty but you'd already gone! Where did you find the diamond that you needed to reconnect the relay?"

"Bridget's watch," Barnaby replied. "We found it on the face of Bridget's watch, after this man pointed it out to us. He was a homeless person whom we met while we were stranded. He was very intelligent and very kind to us."

"Let me see that watch," Dr. Tempus demanded. He took Bridget's watch and examined it carefully. "There's no diamond missing from the face of this watch! See? It looks like it's just been cleaned and polished."

Bridget grabbed the watch. Her eyes widened in amazement. "You're right," she said. "It's in better shape than ever!"

They all looked at each other in stunned silence.

"Well, let's eat!" Barnaby said, eyeing the table of food. "I'm starving!"

The time travelers ate until they thought they would explode. Strangely, besides all the other wonderful dishes Dr. Tempus had prepared, there was a platter of Mouseburger Helper.

Sitting around—indeed, unable to get up—after dinner, they all began to reminisce.

"You know, I'm ready to hang up my time-traveling shoes for a while," Bridget said. "I want to think about all the people we've met, all the places we've seen, all the events we've witnessed. I've learned so much. And now I've got some questions about the present that I want to pursue."

"I think I agree with you," Barnaby replied. "It's time to take a break. I know one thing, though. If I get the chance to do it again, I'll travel that time line like a detective in search of a clue."

"Ah, you Americans are so creative with words," Babette sighed. "I shall miss your verbal ingenuity, but for now I also must return home. I will never forget these adventures. You are my best friends, so count me in when you are ready to hit the history trail again."

"Why, Babette," Bridget laughed, "I think we're beginning to rub off on you!"

A puzzled look crossed Babette's face. "Well, I have absorbed much of your culture," she said. "Just keep Barnaby's socks someplace where they won't 'rub off' on me!"

As they laughed together, Beauregard slipped out of the door unnoticed. He never liked good-byes. They were always too emotional, too sentimental. Besides, he had a strange feeling that they would all be together again soon. After all, they were the best of friends.

Yes, I'm still here, but just for a moment. Now I hope you see why I *love* history! History is not just some boring set of facts that you're supposed to memorize for a test. History is life. History is adventure. History is part of us all. As you grow older, history becomes very personal, very important. In a way, you develop your own sense of time by studying history. So, welcome to the world of history!

✍ FOOD FOR THOUGHT ✍

Now that we've come to the end of our journey together, take out your journal and reread some of your old entries. What did you enjoy the most? What did you enjoy the least? Write down at least five new ideas that you never realized about American history. Remember, they don't have to be facts! Use the facts to create the ideas!

So, did you come up with some good ideas? Write them down in your journal, and save them for a rainy day. You know the kind of day I mean! It's a day when somebody forgets to tell you that you are part of something important. It's a day when you don't quite feel up to par. Read your new ideas again and hopefully, you'll realize just how important you are. You and all of your new ideas are the future. Keep up the excellent work. I know you can do it!

The Presidents of the United States 1789-1992

George Washington, 1789-1797

John Adams, 1797-1801

Thomas Jefferson, 1801-1809

James Madison, 1809-1817

James Monroe, 1817-1825

John Quincy Adams, 1825-1829

Andrew Jackson, 1829-1837

Martin Van Buren, 1837-1841

William Henry Harrison, March 4, 1841-April 4, 1841 (31 days)

John Tyler, 1841-1845

James K. Polk, 1845-1849

Zachary Taylor, 1849-1850 (1 year, 127 days)

Millard Fillmore, 1850-1853 (2 years, 238 days)

Franklin Pierce, 1853-1857

James Buchanan, 1857-1861

Abraham Lincoln, March 4, 1861-April 12, 1865 (4 years, 42 days)

Andrew Johnson, April 15, 1865-March 4, 1869 (3 years, 324 days)

Ulysses S. Grant, 1869-1877

Rutherford B. Hayes, 1877-1881

James A. Garfield, March 4, 1881-September 19, 1881 (199 days)

Chester A. Arthur, September 19, 1881-March 4, 1885 (3 years, 166 days)

Grover Cleveland, 1885-1889

Benjamin Harrison, 1889-1893

Grover Cleveland, 1893-1897

William McKinley, March 4, 1897- September 14, 1901 (4 years, 194 days)

Theodore Roosevelt, September 14, 1901-March 4, 1909 (7 years, 172 days)

William Howard Taft, 1909-1913

Woodrow Wilson, 1913-1921

Warren G. Harding, March 4, 1921-August 2, 1923 (2 years, 151 days)

Calvin Coolidge, August 3, 1923-March 4, 1929 (5 years, 215 days)

Herbert Hoover, 1929-1933

Franklin D. Roosevelt, March 4, 1933-April 12, 1945 (12 years, 39 days)

Harry S. Truman, April 12, 1945-January 20, 1953 (7 years, 283 days)

Dwight D. Eisenhower, 1953-1961

John F. Kennedy, January 20, 1961-November 22, 1963 (2 years, 306 days)

Lyndon B. Johnson, November 22,1963-January 20, 1969 (5 years, 59 days)

Richard M. Nixon, January 20, 1969-August 8, 1974 (5 years, 201 days)

Gerald R. Ford, August 9, 1974-January 20, 1976 (2 years, 164 days)

Jimmy Carter, 1976-1980

Ronald Reagan, 1980-1988

George Bush, 1988-1992

Bill Clinton, 1992-present

Answers

Quiz #1—The Colonists Rule!

1. Patrick Henry; he would rather die than live under the unjust rule of a tyrant.
2. To escape religious persecution in Europe; to create new economic opportunities for themselves, too.
3. Economic opportunity and religious tolerance.
4. The American colonists had no elected representatives in Parliament, Great Britain's law-making body. So, the colonists had no way to voice their approval or disapproval of Britain's plans to tax the colonies. The colonists wanted representatives in Parliament if they were going to be taxed.
5. The Stamp Act
6. The Tea Act of 1773
7. The Intolerable Acts
8. Thomas Paine; to convince the colonists to separate from Great Britain for their own benefit.
9. Benjamin Franklin
10. Thomas Jefferson

Quiz #2—Checking Out Some Important Documents

1. The Bill of Rights
2. The Articles of Confederation
3. James Madison
4. Bicameral
5. Legislative
6. Executive
7. Judicial
8. Judicial review
9. First Amendment
10. The president

Quiz #3—Exploring the New Frontier

1. The Louisiana Purchase
2. Lewis and Clark
3. Sacajawea
4. The War of 1812
5. Tecumseh
6. Andrew Jackson
7. The Trail of Tears
8. James K. Polk
9. Manifest Destiny
10. Texas

Quiz #4— Beauregard's return

1. Fort Sumter, South Carolina
2. 1861-1865; close to 600,000
3. William Lloyd Garrison
4. Missouri Compromise
5. Gettysburg
6. Robert E. Lee
7. Ulysses S. Grant
8. Freedman's Bureau
9. Ku Klux Klan
10. Abraham Lincoln; John Wilkes Booth
11. Harriet Tubman

Quiz #5—Machines!

1. Alexander Graham Bell
2. Garrett Morgan
3. Thomas Alva Edison
4. Henry Ford
5. The Wright Brothers
6. Jan Matzeliger
7. Thomas Alva Edison
8. Henry Ford
9. Alexander Graham Bell
10. Thomas Alva Edison

Quiz #6—The Roaring Twenties and the Depressing Thirties

1. Gertrude Ederle
1. Ellis Island
3. Warren G. Harding
4. Charles Lindbergh
5. Amelia Earhart
6. John Thomas Scopes
7. Franklin Delano Roosevelt
8. October 29, 1929
9. Albert Einstein
10. Walt Disney

Quiz #7—War and Peace: The Forties and Fifties

1. Woodrow Wilson
1. Treaty of Versailles
3. Adolph Hitler
4. Franklin Delano Roosevelt
5. Pearl Harbor
6. Dwight D. Eisenhower
7. Communism
8. Germany, Italy, and Japan
9. Harry S. Truman
10. Joseph Stalin

Quiz #8—Changes: The Sixties and Seventies

1. Rosa Parks
1. Reverend Dr. Martin Luther King, Jr.
3. Cesar Chavez
4. Betty Friedan
5. Wounded Knee
6. Stonewall
7. Richard Nixon
8. Ho Chi Minh
9. *Roe* v. *Wade*
10. *Brown* v. *Board of Education*

Notes

Notes

Notes

Notes

ABOUT THE AUTHOR

Jim Alouf is an associate professor of education at Sweet Briar College in Virginia where he has worked for fifteen years. Prior to completing his Ph.D in social studies at the University of Virginia, Jim taught high school social studies at Middlesex High School, Middlesex, New Jersey for nine years. He completed his M.A. at Rutgers University in Political Theory and his B.A. in Government and Politics at King's College in Wiles-Barre, Pennsylvania. Jim lives in a small country home in Ivy, Virginia near the birthplace of Meriwether Lewis. He loves to travel and enjoys the beauty of his home state, Virginia. Among his favorite interests are teaching, science fiction, airplanes, politics, and history. He hopes that you enjoy reading this book as much as he did writing it!

More Bestselling Smart Junior Titles from The Princeton Review

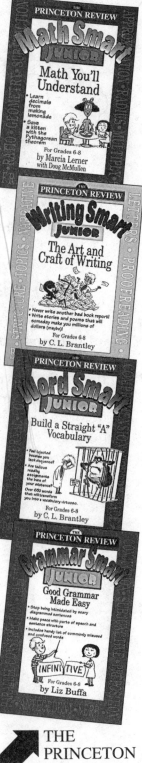

A 1995 Parents Choice Gold Medal Award-Winning Series

Join Barnaby, Babette, Bridget, their fat cat friend Beauregard, and all the crazy people they meet as they travel around the world, across time, and through space in search of adventure and knowledge.

"Educational and entertaining describes this series. The Princeton Review has made learning just plain fun."
—*Writing Teacher* magazine

AMERICAN HISTORY SMART JUNIOR
$12.00 • 0-679-77357-6
A time travel adventure through history!

ASTRONOMY SMART JUNIOR
$12.00 • 0-679-76906-4
Blast off to Mars with the Smart Junior gang.

GEOGRAPHY SMART JUNIOR
$12.00 • 0-679-77522-6
The Smart Junior gang has to solve a mystery by finding clues from all over the world.

GRAMMAR SMART JUNIOR
$12.00 • 0-679-76212-4
Good grammar made easy. Selected by *Curriculum Administrator* magazine readers as one of the Top 100 Products of 1995-96.

MATH SMART JUNIOR
$12.00 • 0-679-75935-2
Save a kitten with the Pythagorean theorem and more! "Learning at its giggliest," says the *Chicago Tribune KIDNEWS.*

WORD SMART JUNIOR
$12.00 • 0-679-75936-0
Build a straight A vocabulary with the Smart Junior gang as they have a crazy adventure with over 650 vocabulary words.

WRITING SMART JUNIOR
$12.00 • 0-679-76131-4
Book reports, school papers, letter writing, story writing and even poetry are covered in *Writing Smart Junior,* selected by The New York Public Library for its 1996 Books for the Teen Age List.

THE PRINCETON REVIEW